THE JOSHUA DILEMMA

MENTORING SERVANT LEADERS TO TRANSITION THROUGH MINISTRY SUCCESSION

DR. RAYFORD E. MALONE

Foreword by Dr. David Hardage

GC2 PRESS

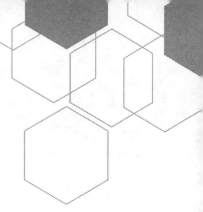

Foreword

"I commend Dr. Ray Malone on addressing well a subject of great importance in today's world, particularly the Church. Even though transition/change is not something most of us enjoy, it can be managed in a positive, Kingdom enhancing manner. And, an early start to a healthy transition begins with a good, active and truly engaged mentorship. Dr. Malone is a good and Godly man and his experience in and out of the Church makes him a wonderful candidate to write on the subject at hand and he does so in the work."

David Hardage
Baptist General Convention of Texas
Executive Director

"Life is a journey, not a destination."
—Ralph Waldo Emerson

Contents

Introduction..7

1. The Leadership Phenomenon.............................9
   The Doer Versus the Leader.................................11
   That's Too Much Power.......................................11
   The Problem With Our Davids............................18

2. Be Thankful for Your Jethros...........................23
   Respect the Person and the Position................25
   What Are You Doing for the People?................28
   Making Mistakes in Ministry.............................30

3. Developing Right Relationships......................37
   It All Starts With Trust..38
   It's All In How You Look At It.............................42
   Ministry Succession: Your Choice or God's Choice............43
   What's Private Should Be Made Public.............50

4. Managing Your Transitions..............................53
   Understanding Change vs Transition...............54
   Room For Growth..57
   Show Time-Visions and Dreams.........................61

5. The Dropped Baton 65

My Actions (and My Non-Actions) Causes Reactions.........66

No Succession...69

Death of a Leader—Not The Death of A Ministry.................71

The Job Is Not Over Until It's Over.....................................73

The Lost Generation..76

6. Passing the Mantle of Leadership.........................83

The Passing of the Mantle..100

The Long Walk of Ministry...102

The Crossover...105

Eye on the Prize...105

Conclusion..111
Decision for Christ..113
Contact...114

Introduction

The Joshua Dilemma is a book about managing transitions within the ministry—specifically the transition of leadership. In this book, we will take an in-depth look at the call and preparation of the next generation of leaders through the eyes of the mentor and the one being mentored.

Through this book, we will learn that as the elder generation prepares for its exodus, it is incumbent that the incoming generation takes hold of the mantle of leadership and continue the work of the Lord without breaks or delays in the forward progress of the church.

Through this book, we will learn that leadership is a fluid concept: meaning no one man or woman will hold the mantle of leadership for very long, and yet their leadership style can cause the ministry to expand or regress according to their capability to inspire others.

Through this book, we will learn that the church's vitality and longevity are directly tied to the strength of our training and mentoring programs within the ministry today. If we fail to properly prepare our replacements, we weaken, and possibly destroy, the very church we say we love. In short, if we have no training or mentoring programs, we fall victim to the Joshua Dilemma which is to say: Who will replace our generation of leaders after we are gone?

Chapter 1

THE LEADERSHIP PHENOMENON

"And what you have heard from me in the presence of many witnesses entrust to faithful men who will be able to teach others also."

—2 Timothy 2:2

"So the LORD said to Moses, 'Take Joshua son of Nun, a man in whom is the spirit of leadership, and lay your hand on him.'"

—Numbers 27:18

"The greatest good you can do for another is not just to share your riches but to reveal to him his own."

—Benjamin Disraeli

Promotion. Succession. These two words, although different, both speak towards the same issue whether in the corporate world or in the established church. That issue is the passing of the mantle of leadership from one person to another in hopes of guiding the next generation into the future. In this book, we will take an in-depth look at the dynamics of leadership through several men of God who were placed under the mantle of leadership and how they handled the process of succession and biblical mentorship.

But first, let's state a simple definition of what leadership is. Leadership is defined as the ability to motivate and encourage others to cause them to focus on a given task. In short form, leadership is simply people management.

Sounds pretty simple, doesn't it? A leader is a person who inspires others to perform given tasks. When we look at leadership in this basic form, we see that anyone who has the power to motivate and encourage can be a leader. A person doesn't need a title or a badge on his shirt to be a leader. A leader is simply someone who inspires.

Later in this book, we will deal with good leadership versus bad leadership, but for now let's keep it simple. Leaders inspire.

The mother who convinces her child to try to sleep through the night without the closet light being on is a leader. The child who helps guide the middle-aged lady across the street is a leader. The Boy Scout who stands in front of his troop and recites the Boy Scout pledge is a leader. For many of us, when we think of strong leadership, we look towards people we admire. For instance, we may look towards pastors of megachurches or leaders of industry, but many of us fail to identify the leadership skills that are shaped day by day in our own homes and neighborhoods.

Now if leadership is defined as the ability to motivate and encourage others to cause them to focus on a given task (people management), then the leader must be the person who possesses this ability. The Bible teaches us that God has given each of us individual spiritual talents (Ephesians 4:8) to use for His glory, but He has also given us individual natural talents for the same purpose.

There are some people who possess the natural desire to be leaders. However, there are many who misuse these talents. The drug dealer can be a leader just as the judge or the policeman. Understand, it is not the desire to lead others that's bad, but it's what our desires, good or bad, cause us to do as we lead others.

The Doer Versus the Leader

My intent in writing this book is to uncover, teach, and ultimately model what godly committed leadership is in respect to ministry advancement and ministry succession. However, to do this, we must define the difference between the " doer" mentality and the "leader" mentality.

Good leadership is not only a benefit for the leader, but it is a benefit for the staff or church leadership. The reason for this is simple. Both parties must be active in the leadership process. When one party is active and the other isn't you automatically fall under the covering of bad leadership.

On an individual basis, bad leadership can destroy a person's purpose, vision, and destiny. The worst part of bad leadership is that it can destroy the purpose, vision, and destiny of the people God has assigned you to lead.

So let's start by discussing the "doer" mentality. Many of us are more familiar with this mentality than we think. If you've ever been around a person who has to "do it all" then you've experienced the "doer" mentality. A "doer" is the leader who does all the work while everyone else watches and waits for the leader to complete tasks that are designed for group participation. Leaders who possess this mentality usually find their ministries filled with bad decisions and missed ministry opportunities.

Many leaders, today, do not understand that leadership is a group phenomenon. The leader must have interpersonal influence and personal power. Simply put, the leader must have the power of persuasion. But, here's the problem with many leaders today: Once they move into leadership and they see they hold power and authority over people, ministries, or companies, some become petty in their thinking. When this happens, many seek to hold the power for self-glorification instead of the Godly mandate they've been assigned, and ultimately, they destroy lives instead of building them.

That's Too Much Power

I remember watching the movie *Malcolm X* starring Denzel Washington. There was an early scene in the movie where Denzel leads the Fruit of

Islam (bodyguards) in a march to a local hospital after one of its members was brutally beaten. After making sure the injured man would survive at the moment of their disbursement, Malcolm X (Washington) made a slight hand gesture and the Fruit of Islam formed ranks and marched off. After seeing this demonstration of power the police captain said, "That's too much power for one man to have."

For many leaders, the seductive authority of power is like a drug. The more power given to a person the greater their sense of responsibility will be or the more depraved they will become. Proverbs 29:2 says, "When the righteous are in authority, the people rejoice; But when a wicked man rules, the people groan."

If this Scripture was ever put to the test it was proven during the life of King Saul. He is the one person who would have gained tremendous wisdom if he understood Luke 12:48: "For everyone, to whom much is given, from him much will be required; and to whom much has been committed, of him they will ask the more."

However, like many men, Saul stopped looking at this power as God-given authority to bless the people of God, and he began seeing it as a tool to be used for his amusement, gain, or weapon.

In the corporate world, as well as in the church, when bad leadership is in place the whole organization struggles. In First Samuel 14:24-25, we see Saul issuing a very foolish command thus demonstrating his poor leadership skills. Although they were in a time of war, he had commanded his army not to taste any food until the evening so his great anger would be fulfilled. Can you imagine the physical activity and strength to fight from sunup to sundown all the while chasing your enemy across barren wastelands and wooded forests? Can you imagine having to do all this without the opportunity to eat to gain nourishment for your depleted energy?

I must submit to you that any leader who desires to lead his staff or church correctly will do whatever they can not to distress their workers. To distress their workers means they have made them to suffer or experience unnecessary pain of some kind in the work area.

When this happens, many leaders begin to quickly lose the support of their staff because if the staff can't trust you then why should they follow you?

In this sense, King Saul is like many of today's typical leaders. He was a big man physically, but he had "small man syndrome." He carried a chip on his shoulder throughout his kingship, and he never forgave a wound, nor did he forgive who gave it to him. His "chip" led him to constantly fight battle after battle and eventually it destroyed his family. His "chip" caused him to take his life on a battlefield with his son Jonathan, and it even caused several of his grandchildren to be killed for his war crimes.

Throughout his life, King Saul never matured as a leader although he had many opportunities. At best, he was a poor leader who loved to fight when the odds were in his favor, but when he felt vulnerable or exposed, he would cower and allow others to fight his battles.

As a leader, Saul was given a golden opportunity to lead by example and kill Goliath, but he rebelled because of his own personal view of himself. Although Saul was physically larger than everyone else in the tribes he still felt small in his own eyes. God knew it, Samuel knew it, and Saul knew it. In First Samuel 15:17, as God is ripping the kingdom out of the hands of Saul, He speaks to this poor characteristic through Samuel. The text says, "When you were little in your own eyes, were you not head of the tribes of Israel? And did not the LORD anoint you king over Israel?"

Small Man Syndrome isn't entirely about size. It's more common among leaders who are petty.

Who wants to follow a leader who's small in his own eyes? Who wants to follow a leader who says, "Do as I say, but not as I do?" This is one of the worst forms of leadership because it shows your subordinates that you expect them to bleed for you but you won't bleed for them. Sure you might be saying, "Hold on preacher! Wasn't Saul a man of war?" And the answer to the question is yes. But keep in mind that true leaders do not get to select what wars they fight. They don't get to pick and choose their battles. True leaders understand that if God has set the stage for you to kill a Goliath then you must kill your Goliath. Keep in mind, leaders, you must climb every mountain that God places in your path whether you like it or not.

Leaders must understand that the power needed to climb their mountains doesn't lie in us but in God. David, who was physically small but spiritually big, accessed this power in God and he slew a giant. Saul, who was physically big but spiritually small, denied this power and he lost the right to lead the entire nation.

When you compare their size, Saul did not measure up to Goliath's physical stature, but if there was anyone that was close it would have been Saul. Scripture teaches us that Saul was head and shoulders (height wise) above any other man in Israel. First Samuel 10:23 states, "So they ran and brought him from there; and when he (Saul) stood among the people, he was taller than any of the people from his shoulders upward. And Samuel said to all the people, 'Do you see him whom the Lord has chosen, that there is no one like him among all the people?'"

From reading this Scripture, we see Saul had the physical size of a king, but he lacked the leadership qualities of a king.

Saul lacked the conviction of a true leader because he led the people of God by his emotions and not by his responsibilities. When you begin to do some self-analysis you will find that many people lead by their emotions and not their responsibilities. Our fear, anger, and hatred are strong motivating forces, but they will all fall short because they are not the true foundation for leadership decisions. Emotional decision -making might save you once or twice, but more times than not it's a curse because it lacks sound wisdom. This is why a true leader doesn't lead out of his emotions. He leads out of his responsibilities.

Emotional leaders react. Responsible leaders respond. Sometimes they might look the same, but trust me, there's a big difference between the two. To react means you move instinctively without forethought or assessment. To respond means you've reasoned your response and calculated its outcome.

Saul was a leader who led by his emotions, and it showed he was a terrible leader. Yes, he was a valiant warrior, but a leader has to be much more than a fighter. He must lead his team with his eyes firmly focused on God and on his mission. In this referenced text, we see that Saul led out of his anger and in so doing it caused his troops to be malnourished and unprepared for the battle that was to come.

When we look at the authority of Saul, we see that he was, without question, the leader of the people. Although his order proved disastrous to his army they followed his command. This lets us know that all leaders, because of their position alone, are able to speak blessings or curses into the lives of those who follow them.

This is why we must have trained leaders as well as mature leaders. Notice that in this text these men were afraid of breaking the law of Saul, but they did not care one bit about breaking the law of God.

These men expected Saul to lead them correctly. In today's workplace and church, I've heard many leaders tell their staff to throw the rule book out the window and follow their lead, often to their detriment. I believe we see this more in the church than in the workplace because church people are faster to operate in blind faith and say, "This is God's chosen vessel. He won't steer us wrong." This is the worst mindset to have because it gives the selfish leader the room he needs to damage and often times destroy the faith of the members in that church or department.

In my life, I have learned there's only one person who I am supposed to have blind faith in and that's God. Everyone else will be questioned.

In the last two decades of preaching, I've heard pastors tell their congregations, "Do not worry about reading your Bibles. I'm your leader. God will tell me what we should do." If you belong to any church or ministry where the leader talks like this I submit to you it's time to look for another church or ministry – fast! This is the mindset of satan himself.

As a pastor and leader, I have learned that the church and workplace function best when we're all transparent and on the same page. One thing I often say to the church and staff I lead is to re-read and study everything I preach about. I do not expect anyone I've led to get to Heaven and tell God, "Well, Pastor Malone said…" No. I tell them they must read and study the

Word of God for themselves. This is why Second Timothy 2:15 teaches us to " study to show thyself approved" because each man is responsible for his own soul.

Second, although it was a bad leadership decision on Saul's part, we see that the people were still held accountable to the command. According to the law, they were supposed to slaughter the animals and allow them to hang upside down from a tree so that the blood would drain out of the body before consuming them. However, the Scripture says they were so hungry they slaughtered and maimed some of the animals on the ground, and they ate the flesh raw which was a terrible sin before God.

To remove the sin of the people, we see Saul building an altar before God, but instead of praying for the sins of the people, he prayed for God to allow him to continue pursuing his enemies (I Samuel 14:37).

This shows another ding in the armor of Saul's leadership. In this moment, Saul could have risen to the occasion before God and repented of his hasty order and pled for the people; but his personal agenda was too great and he took the entire country along for the ride with him.

As Saul commanded, the people had no choice but to follow. The priest had already consented by giving his permission; however, this time God was not on board with the actions of Saul or His people so God did not heed his prayer. To elicit an answer from God, Saul asked God to direct him to the person who broke his command by casting lots and the lot fell to Jonathan who, although innocent because he did not know the command of Saul, was guilty because he was a man under the authority of Saul and thereby was sentenced to death.

Does this paint a true picture of the poor leadership skills of Saul? In First Samuel chapter 15, God commanded Saul to destroy the Amalekites for their trespasses against the children of Israel. According to God's command, Saul was to utterly destroy the people and all of their livestock. However, after the battle, Saul spared Agag and some of the choice animals. This led God to express his deep regret for the leadership of Saul to Samuel: "I greatly regret that I have set up Saul as king, for he has turned back from following Me, and has not performed My commandments."

Now, here is the irony of this situation. God commanded Saul to destroy the Amalekites and everything they possessed; however, Saul spared the life of King Agag. But when it comes to Saul issuing the command that no one was to eat before evening he was prepared to kill his son for tasting some honey. What kind of leader is so focused on his own glory that he can't freely admit that his order was a mistake? When Samuel confronted Saul about his sin in First Samuel 15, Saul begged for forgiveness. However, when it came to his son's sin he desired full payment and he sought to kill his own son.

So tell me what kind of leader was Saul? What kind of leader denies his staff the opportunity to eat freely from the blessings that flow from the land of milk and honey?

Can you imagine seeing the wondrous sight while in the midst of your deepest hunger? Some theologians believe the armies of the Philistines broke open the honeycombs as they fled before the armies of Israel in an effort to escape Saul's wrath. Or maybe God supernaturally allowed this honey to fall on the ground before these hungry men so that Saul could see that God was giving them the necessary blessing they would need to have their greatest victory possible. If this is God's work, can you perceive the spiritual significance of being in a land flowing with "milk and honey," but because of the command of your leader you can't taste of the blessings that God has allowed to fall at your feet? Do you think these men were groaning internally because of the view of the honey on the ground and the fear of breaking Saul's command?

Jonathan spoke about this foolish command in First Samuel 14:29-30 when he said, "My father has troubled the land. Look now, how my countenance has brightened because I tasted a little of this honey. How much better if the people had eaten freely today of the spoil of their enemies which they found! For now would there not have been a much greater slaughter among the Philistines?"

In this instance, we see bad leadership has not only slowed the people, it has caused them to sin, and it has damaged their victory in their promised land. However, in a young Jonathan, we see a right thinking leader because he understands what it would take to maximize their victory.

Remember, Saul was a man who led by his emotions, and now we see Jonathan looking at leadership through the eyes of responsibility.

When Jonathan assessed the situation he measured the needs of the men, as well as their strengths and weaknesses against his personal desire for total victory. Unlike his father, he was looking to do what was best for the men he led instead of doing what was best for himself.

As we look at the effect of Saul's foolish command we see that it might have saved the Israelites a few minutes in pursuing their enemies, but it caused them defilement in the long run. As leaders, we must understand that there will always be "quick fixes" in ministry and life, but ultimately, if it causes you to drift from God no "fix" is ever good enough.

The Problem With Our Davids

When God allowed David to begin finding favor in the hearts of the people, we see a steady decrease in Saul's leadership skills. From the moment Saul heard "Saul has killed his thousands, and David his ten thousands," Saul was fixed on destroying David. The Bible tells us several times that Saul tried to kill David by throwing his javelin at David or pursuing David with his army. The Bible also instructs us that Saul was so desperate to kill David that he began trying to manipulate his son to go along with him in his quest.

First Samuel 20:30-33 says, "Then Saul's anger was aroused against Jonathan, and he said to him, 'You son of a perverse, rebellious woman! Do I not know that you have chosen the son of Jesse to your own shame and to the shame of your mother's nakedness? For as long as the son of Jesse lives on the earth, you shall not be established, nor your kingdom. Now therefore, send and bring him to me, for he shall surely die.' And Jonathan answered Saul his father, and said to him, 'Why should he be killed? What has he done?' Then Saul cast a spear at him to kill him, by which Jonathan knew that it was determined by his father to kill David."

Did you see that? Since Saul could not kill David personally or entice his son to betray David, he tried to use another tactic that men in leadership often use, and that is manipulation. From the first moment of their relationship, Jonathan and David were close. The Bible goes so far as to say their souls were knit together, and Saul tried to sever their spiritual connection by offering his son the one thing Saul desperately desired: the kingdom.

When it comes to leaders who seek to manipulate others, we must understand their "offerings" are always rooted in the things they desire for themselves. Saul wanted the kingdom, but Jonathan wanted a right relationship with David, and it almost cost him his life.

When people who seek to manipulate you find that they can't do so, they will often times turn on you, and the emotion they used to draw you close to them is the same emotion they will use to push you away. Ultimately, they will take a "me against the world" philosophy, and if you are not with them, in their eyes, you can move from being a friend to a foe in an instant.

This biblical example shows us that Saul's lust for David's life was rooted in another emotion: jealousy.

When we look at the words of Saul, he says "as long as the son of Jesse lives on the earth, you shall not be established, nor your kingdom." Every leader who holds a position needs to understand this central truth about God, and that is, God is the only one who knows what the future holds. Yes, it is incumbent for us to prepare our children for the best future we can provide, but it is up to God where He sends them to fulfill their purpose.

I don't believe for one second that Saul was really looking out for what was best for Jonathan. I believe Saul only said these words to entice Jonathan to bring David to his table so he could kill him. Why do I believe this? Because if Saul was truly concerned about Jonathan's kingdom he wouldn't have tried to kill him. The text says when Jonathan tried to defend David, Saul hurled a spear at him. "Then Saul cast a spear at him to kill him, by which Jonathan knew that it was determined by his father to kill David."

The same way Saul determined to kill David was the same way Saul determined to kill his own son.

Many leaders would never say they maintain this view but they do especially in the church. Many pastors and ministry leaders refuse to train the next generation of leaders to the detriment of the whole church ministry. Instead of planning for the future, the "doer" seeks to plan for today. They want to teach all the classes and they are very watchful over their churches because they do not trust their leadership.

This is one reason many pastors and leaders never take vacations. They are so paranoid that something will change that they can never enjoy what God has blessed them to oversee.

We must remember that the body of Christ is a living organism and as such it needs to grow and expand. As leaders in the church and the secular world, we must seek to train ourselves "out of a job," meaning, we need to train our replacements to do our jobs better than we do so that God can release us to move on to our next job assignment.

In today's world, too many self-important leaders seek to hoard power. They believe once they are on the top of the mountain (and they never get there), they should push everyone else off. However, after so many years of trying to reach the top of the mountain they realize at the last minute their time has run out, and they don't have anyone to take their place.

A third negative emotion that Saul used was humiliation. In his rant, Saul called his son a bastard. He said, "You son of a perverse, rebellious woman!" If that wasn't enough he then tried to humiliate him further by calling him a traitor to the crown when he said, "Do I not know that you have chosen the son of Jesse to your own shame and to the shame of your mother's nakedness?" Then, finally, he called his son a fool when he said, "For as long as the son of Jesse lives on the earth, you shall not be established, nor your kingdom."

In today's world, many bad leaders use these tactics as weapons to entice people to do as they ask. However, although these can be useful at times, they are not the correct way true leaders should seek to lead their teams or churches. A true leader seeks to inspire and build rather than force obedience by belittling people and tearing them down.

STUDY GUIDE

Chapter 1: The Leadership Phenomenon

1. Are you a "doer" or a "leader"? Give three examples of who you lead and how you lead them. Do you train your staff or your congregation?

2. How do you view the "power" that's been assigned to you? Do you love being able to tell others what to do? Do you think you are free to speak to people any way you like because you have a position? Do you lead with a soft voice or a loud voice?

3. When you speak to people do you seek to encourage them or do you seek to manipulate them? Share a story of a time when you were encouraged to do better. Now share a story where someone tried to manipulate you into doing what they wanted. What was your response to both?

4. What mistakes in leadership have you made lately? How did you recover from them? Why did you make the mistakes? Did you allow God to speak through you? Did you speak from your emotions or from your heart?

5. Look back over your life and identify three mentors who you admire. Now share what qualities they possessed that you admire. Do you have these qualities? Why or why not? Are you seeking ways to build these qualities within yourself?

Chapter 2

BE THANKFUL FOR YOUR JETHROS

"Let every person be in subjection to the governing authorities. For there is no authority except from God, and those which exist are established by God."
—Romans 13:1

"There is nothing worse for a young convert than to be thrust into leadership without mentoring and ongoing coaching because the devil relishes these vulnerable souls."

—Gary Rohrmayer

Did you know Moses had to learn to be a leader? If you look closely at his life you can actually see Moses move from a "doer" to a "leader." It's true. When Moses began leading the Israelites out of Egypt he was operating in a "doer" mentality, and it wasn't until his father-in-law came to visit him that he saw his mistakes in leadership.

This is why we must be thankful for our Jethroes. You see, Jethro represents people we trust who have been where we are trying to go. They are our mentors who have leadership skills themselves, and they constantly pour into our lives in an effort to inspire the next generation to maximize every gift they possess for the glory of God.

If you were seeking marital advice would you ask a person who has been divorced ten times? I sure wouldn't because it's obvious they struggle with marriage, and their issues have led them to quit several times along the way. Sure, the beauty of marriage causes them to say, "I do"; but the issues in marriage cause them to say, "I don't." Likewise, when it comes to leadership, you want to receive advice from people you trust, people who have been in the fire, endured the fire, and ultimately, made it through the fire.

When Moses wandered to the back side of the desert he found everything he needed at Jethro's house. Moses found substance, a wife, a job, and a father figure under the covering of Jethro. Moses had lived the life of an imposter in Egypt, and when he fled across the desert, the only place he found refuge was in Jethro's tents. So it would be natural for Jethro to be able to speak into Moses' life as a mentor because he had earned a high level of trust.

In Jethro, Moses found someone who cared about him and, more importantly, someone who didn't judge him.

Can you imagine an exhausted, tired, mangy Moses showing up on your doorstep and you have to make the decision whether or not to allow him to come inside your place of security? Can you grasp the weight of the decision Jethro had to make when he was shown Moses and then told that Moses had defended his daughters from men seeking to mistreat them?

This is what Jethro had to ponder as he saw Moses. In my mind, I see Moses as a man who came with nothing. However, this glimmer of strong character caused Jethro to give him a chance which eventually led Moses to become his son-in-law and trusted friend.

This is how many of us come to our spiritual mentors. We come with nothing, yet God allows our mentors to see the potential in each of us.

When we are birthed into the ministry or a new position on our jobs we aren't prepared to operate on any level in God, so He assigns mentors in our pathway. Just as Moses was unprepared to live in the desert environment, many of us are unprepared to operate in a ministry environment. Moses was driven from Egypt because he murdered an Egyptian. Most mentors, especially in the church, understand if you show up on their doorstep something is driving you there.

Many mentees don't know what this driving force is, but most mentors do. The driving force is the accumulation of your emotions, mistakes, and bad choices that send you on a quest for someone to help make sense of it all. At the time you are going through all this, you don't recognize that God is still directing your path, nor do you know where He is sending you. All you knew was you needed help finding your way. If this is you, press on! One day you will stand before your Jethro. Pray that they see something in you worth shaping, developing, and protecting.

For the mentors, they simply see a younger version of themselves. This alone is enough reason for the mentor to open his heart and his life to help the mentee find his purpose in God.

Respect the Person and the Position

There's no worse leader than one who demands respect from others but never gives respect to his church, family, or staff.

Upon leaving Egypt, it took the Israelites less than fifteen days to go from the Wilderness of Sin to the border of Mount Sinai. Somewhere in this two week journey we see the arrival of Jethro with his daughter, Moses' wife Zipporah, and their children. From the beginning of chapter eighteen we see the high regard Moses had for Jethro. In verse seven, it says, "So Moses went out to meet his father-in-law, bowed down, and kissed him. And they asked each other about their well-being, and they went into the tent."

Although Moses was the leader of this vast multitude, he still took the time to pay homage to his mentor. The King James uses the word "obeisance" which means a movement of the body expressing deep respect or deferential courtesy, as before a superior; a bow, curtsy, or other similar gesture. In this, we see Moses giving honor to whom honor was due. First Timothy 5:17 says, "Let the elders who rule well be counted worthy of double honor, especially those who labor in the word and doctrine."

Second, we see Moses paying homage to Jethro when he allowed him to lead in the evening sacrifice and feast. Verse 12 says, "Then Jethro, Moses' father-in-law, took a burnt offering and other sacrifices to offer to God. And

Aaron came with all the elders of Israel to eat bread with Moses' father-in-law before God."

Keep in mind Jethro was the first spiritual leader Moses followed, and like Moses, he had many responsibilities. He was the priest of Midian (Exodus 18:1), and the CEO of the family business, which meant he had to provide for everyone under both coverings: The spiritual and the secular. This included the church and all its responsibilities as well as his workers, wives and daughters.

Did Moses and Jethro deal with the same struggles?

No, they did not, but this is the thing about leadership: Leadership is a universal concept. You might not deal with the same scenarios, but it carries the same formulas.

If you are the leader of a corporation, how do you deal with a disgruntled employee? You go to your company's policies and procedures and you follow them. In the same manner, if you are the leader of a church, how do you deal with a disgruntled church member? You go to your church's policies and procedures, normally called church by-laws, and you follow them. If you are a parent, how do you deal with a disgruntled child? You go to the disciplinary processes you have established with your spouse and you follow them.

See, different scenarios but same basic principles.

Let's take a look at Exodus 18:13-4. "And so it was, on the next day, that Moses sat to judge the people; and the people stood before Moses from morning until evening. So when Moses' father-in-law saw all that he did for the people, he said, 'What is this thing that you are doing for the people? Why do you alone sit, and all the people stand before you from morning until evening?'"

Although Moses had led the children of Israel out of Egypt with a mighty hand, they still had issues that the leadership needed to oversee. The text begins with Moses being positioned to judge over four million Israelites who left Egypt.

Now, as we begin to ponder this thought, we see a startling fact. Here is Moses, the friend of God, as the only judge about to oversee the disputes of over approximately 2.4 million people without any help. Doesn't this sound like the "doer" mentality?

Can you imagine being the only judge with a caseload encompassing approximately 2.4 million people? That's equivalent to the population of Houston. Could you see yourself having to hear dispute after dispute from sunup to sundown?

Can you imagine the weight of that burden? I know I can't. But, nevertheless, Moses tried. Verse 13 says, "Moses sat to judge the people; and the people stood before Moses from morning until evening."

Would you like to stand all day waiting for the only judge? I wouldn't. One of the quickest ways to lose your staff, church, or ministry is to allow the spirit of boredom to creep in. It is better for us to keep our staff focused on the next mission or goal rather than allowing them to mill around and lose their edge for ministry due to boredom while waiting to speak to an unavailable leader.

This is what Moses was facing until he allowed a fellow leader to pour sound wisdom into his life. Yes, Moses stood strong before Pharaoh, but this was a new situation in a new season, and he needed new wisdom in dealing with this new problem in judging the people.

This should show us leaders a startling revelation of the spirit.

No matter how good you are in one area of leadership there is always some place where you will need help. Also, the imagery of this text shows us Moses "sat and the people stood." Now, let's understand this dynamic. Moses is sitting but the people are standing, and this is never good for the body of Christ.

Whenever, as a pastor, you assume the "seat of power," you should expect others to critically judge your position. Although Moses is sitting, he is working, but because of his physical position, many will assume that he is doing very little if anything. And it is the same with you as a pastor. Some will think you spend all your time sitting on your backside enjoying the lap of luxury the church has provided. They do not understand the work, time, or effort that it takes to run a ministry or a business because they are not in your seat.

This is why many co-workers and ministry assistants quickly become weary and despondent as they become tired of standing around all day with nothing to do. However, for these leaders to assume their "seat of power" in the future, they should seek to stand beside their Moses so they can be mentored properly. This way, they learn what it means to do the grunt work before they lead their own troops.

What Are You Doing for the People?

When Moses' father-in-law began to ask questions it was not to put Moses on the spot, but it was to make Moses come to the realization that he could not do it all by himself. This is the job of mentors. They help us think through problems. Mentors are guides to help us think about our processes as they help shine light on the weak areas of our ministries.

The Bible says, "So when Moses' father-in-law saw all that he did for the people, he said, 'What is this thing that you are doing for the people? Why do you alone sit, and all the people stand before you from morning until evening?'" Jethro knew that Moses was performing a great service to the people. Many men and women with the "doer" mentality are great workers, but they need to be shown that in their best moment of working singularly in ministry they are a detriment to the whole body.

Many times when a person with a "doer" mentality sees something that needs to be done they are all over it. But when the "doer" is also the leader, every time he stops and jumps on a new task it brings the entire engine to a screeching halt. This is what Moses was facing. With 2.4 million people, there was no way he could listen to all the issues, arguments, and fights amongst the people. But still he tried.

Every time we try to function as doers instead of leaders, we sabotage our ministries, and we bring all our forward progress to a standstill. This is why we must be thankful for our Jethros. They seek to save us from making mistakes.

Let's look at Moses' reply to Jethro. "Because the people come to me to inquire of God. When they have a difficulty, they come to me, and I judge between one and another; and I make known the statutes of God and His laws."

One of the fastest ways to determine if your employer or ministry head is a "doer" or a "leader" comes when you discover how they view their work. When Jethro asked for Moses' view, he took personal ownership over a shared problem.

A "doer" will always take possession of the issue as if it's his treasure, but a leader will share the wealth of the issue by asking the group for aid in dealing with the issue.

Many pastors and leaders do this. They think that they have to come up with the answers on how to increase work productivity. They think that they have to figure out how to increase membership into Sunday school. They think they have to be the last one to leave the church because someone else might mess up the alarm codes.

Remember, leadership is about the group, not the individual.

Let's take a look at these words Moses uses. "They come to me (for leadership)" and "I (teach them God's ways)." Is there no one else who could have helped Moses with these problems? I am sure somebody would have helped Moses if Moses had asked for it. But since he was used to doing all the work, the worker- bees were content to let him do all the work.

When in doubt, ask! Who says you have to come up with all the ideas or all the answers? No one can operate under those types of expectations, so what are you trying to prove? To stop being a "doer" you must train your mind to think like a "leader."

Remember, leaders, you have to lead them. If you don't teach your followers your vision and instruct them in the way the ministry needs to operate, how can they fulfill their purpose in your ministry? Crisp communication is mandatory when it comes to sharing your vision. You must share your vision with those you are trying to lead. If you don't, you will never be a leader.

Making Mistakes in Ministry

Everybody makes mistakes in ministry. The only " bad" mistake is the one we fail to learn from. In this journey of ministry and life, every leader will have some "oops" moments during their tenure. No one is perfect and nobody gets it right all the time. However, when we see an area that needs to be corrected we must do so as soon as possible.

Let's look at verses 17-19: "The thing that you do is not good. Both you and these people who are with you will surely wear yourselves out. For this thing is too much for you; you are not able to perform it by yourself. Listen now to my voice; I will give you counsel, and God will be with you: Stand before God for the people, so that you may bring the difficulties to God."

When Jethro began speaking to Moses he spoke to him as a father and mentor. He spoke to him as one who was looking out for everyone's best interest, not just his son-in-law's. Notice he refers to the taxation of the situation on Moses and the people. Now this is a leader! Leaders do not take sides. They look toward the benefit of the whole and what will be best for all parties involved.

Relationships like this are few and far between, but if you are able to establish one, I strongly suggest you cherish it because people usually avoid these types of relationships. In most cases, we avoid them because many of us feel they make us vulnerable, but in truth, they make us stronger. Paul said in 1 Corinthians 4:15, "For though you might have ten thousand instructors in Christ, yet you do not have many fathers; for in Christ Jesus I have begotten you through the gospel."

On the dedication page of my previous book, *Everybody Can't Climb This Mountain*, I listed several names of people who I love and recognize as my fathers and mentors in the ministry. This was not written to shame my paternal father. He is a great man who is full of wisdom. But for me to grow in ministry, I had to have men who would teach me how to see through spiritual eyes so that I could become the man of God He had destined for me to become.

Galatians 4:1 says, "Now I say that the heir, as long as he is a child, does not differ at all from a slave, though he is master of all, but is under guardians and stewards until the time appointed by the father." When I was born into ministry on my twenty-fifth birthday I had no idea what was ahead of me. According to this spiritual promise, I am an heir of God, and I am to receive all of His wonderous blessings, but since I was immature in Christ I was looked at as a slave. See, I was counted this way because I didn't fully know Christ. He knew all of me but I did not know all of Him, so He put me under guardians and stewards until I was mature enough to walk in the totality of my calling.

Of the men listed at the beginning of the book, each one, in his special way, has helped me become the man of God I am today. Some covered me for years, some covered me with spiritual conversations, and some covered me with learning how to move and operate in a spirit of excellence.

Another leadership nugget that needs to be pointed out is Jethro never told Moses what to do. For all the advice, he never pushed Moses to do what he suggested. Jethro simply said, "Listen now to my voice; I will give you counsel, and God will be with you." He is in effect saying, let me offer you some advice but in the end you make your own decision. Jethro could have said, "Now, look here Moses! You do what I tell you to do. Remember, I was the one who took care of you when you didn't have a pot to pee in! I was the one who gave you a job. I let you eat at my table. And I even let your dusty behind marry my daughter so YOU do what I say!"

Manipulative leaders are the worst . Like Saul, they want to minimize you and your efforts, seeking to make you feel powerless while they try to make themselves all-powerful.

Jethro's position as a mentor and father to Moses was to give information and advice. He never desired to make this decision for Moses nor did he pressure him. He simply presented a second option, and he allowed Moses to make up his mind.

In many ways, this shows a mature leadership style that's lacking in many churches today. Notice when Jethro gave advice he did not seek to influence Moses either way. In this, we see the wisdom of Jethro as he allowed Moses to decide which action was best for him and the people.

Many times, when a person desires to influence your decisions, he will say, "Well, I think you should." Or, "This is what I would do." By them doing so, you automatically know this is a person who is seeking to control your decision-making process. When you come across such a person, please disqualify them as your mentor.

In verse 20, Jethro gives Moses a plan of wisdom and it all centers on the group phenomenon. First, the leader must be a strong teacher with the ability to inspire and influence his followers to remain focused on what's important. This is why Jethro made sure Moses knew it was his responsibility to teach the people the oracles of God and how they should live their lives when he said, "The statutes and the laws, and show them the way."

So how did Moses do this? He followed a very simple three point plan. He taught them, he trained them, and finally, he trusted them. "Moreover you shall select from all the people able men, such as fear God, men of truth, hating covetousness; and place such over them to be rulers of thousands, rulers of hundreds, rulers of fifties, and rulers of tens. And let them judge the people at all times."

Leadership is a group phenomenon. But in understanding this, we must also understand that we must have the right type of people in leadership. Even Jesus had a Judas. We must select leaders based on their character as individuals and not because we have personal relationships with them. We must select moralistic men who will do the right thing and make the hard decisions when necessary. This selection process in not based on what they look like, but it should be based on the quality of the individuals.

When Christ selected His first four disciples He selected two sets of brothers: Peter and Andrew; James and John. Christ selected these four men because of their character and integrity. When Scripture details these brothers, we find both sets working diligently submitting to the authority of their fathers as fishermen.

Keep in mind that although they possessed strong character, each one had different issues. Who doesn't? Everybody has issues, and just so you know, possessing issues isn't a show- stopper in Christ. He simply seeks men with strong character who will allow Him to hone them, shape them, and finally, mold them into His leadership team.

Finally, Jethro showed Moses the need for him to get his rest and to share his authority with the men who walked with him and who carried a like spirit. Jethro made this point to Moses when he said, "So it will be easier for you, for they will bear the burden with you.   If you do this thing, and God so commands you, then you will be able to endure, and all this people will also go to their place in peace."

In my twenty years of ministry, I've learned there's no greater burden for a pastor than trying to do ministry with men and women who have a contrary spirit. In all honesty, it doesn't matter what facet of ministry it is. It could be on the business side or the ministry side; it doesn't matter. When you are working with people who have their own agendas it brings the ministry to a crawl.

This is why when some members leave the ministry you shouldn't be sad; you should be glad. There are many blessings that come when people say goodbye. With this in mind, when we develop good, solid, Godly leaders it benefits all parties involved.

As a pastor, a chaplain, a husband, a father, a brother, and a business owner, I must get my rest. When I'm not rested too many things suffer. When I used to operate as a "doer," I had a "press my way through" attitude. Whenever I had to be at Bible study and I was dead tired, I would "press my way through." When I was up at midnight working on my doctorate even though sleepy, I would "press my way through." When I had to go and support the various ministries of the church and I was physically sick, I had to "press my way through."

Sure, I had associate ministers who could have taught Bible study. Sure, I could have called it a night and done my homework over the weekend. And, yes, I could have stayed at home in the bed and gotten my rest, but, hey, I was the pastor, right? So I just kept "pressing my way through."

That was fine until I hit a brick wall called failing health and that was something I couldn't "press my way through."

Actually, my "press my way through" attitude ended with me in the hospital.

I remember I got home around 4:00 p.m. and I immediately went to bed. My wife came in and checked on me once, but I vaguely remembered it, and before I knew it, my alarm clock was going off at 6:00 a.m. When I tried to get up, my body refused to cooperate and I found myself in the doctor's office that morning leaving with more medicine than I care to think about . Then I remembered my mother's words: "Ray, learn to work smarter, not harder." That's when I decided to be a leader instead of a "doer."

If you are a "doer" and you decide to keep "pressing your way through," you'll either end up in a body bag, wheel chair, or loony bin. Keep in mind your health is vitally important to your ministry.

This will be my last word on Moses and Jethro. After Moses moved from a "doer" to a "leader," it still took the children of God a while to get used to the change in operation. For many of those under our leadership, we must maintain a mindset that with each change in our perspectives it causes greater change to those who serve under us.

You are not truly a leader until those who follow you follow for the right reasons.

When a new leader rolls out an idea, it takes time for the people to come aboard. Usually, when a leader presents something new the staff and co-workers respond in three ways. First, is compliance. When people comply they will go along with the request. They have non-personal acceptance meaning they will support the leader but from a distance. They have an "if it works, great. If not, who cares" attitude. Second, is resistance. When people disagree with the leader's attempt and they will actively or passively resist it, meaning when you make the suggestion, they disagree with you openly or privately but they will ultimately fight against it. Third, is acceptance. These are the people who quickly get on board and accept the influence from the leader willingly.

The Bible teaches us that the men Moses put in place were faithful, and they were committed to the shared vision they had been given by Moses. Each man oversaw his portion of the Israelite population, and the people were not taxed because Moses shared his power and authority. So I ask you: are you willing to share your power and authority? If not, you are a "doer." If you are willing to share, you're a "leader."

Study Guide

Chapter 2: Be Thankful For Your Jethros

1. Have you identified your Jethro? If not, take a few minutes and think of the persons God has placed in your path who have helped you when you didn't deserve it. Now write down their names and share some of your feelings about them in the moment they helped you.

2. Can you share a time when your Jethro helped you out of a bad situation in life? Can you discuss how their wisdom helped you to be a better person?

3. As you transitioned from a "doer" to a "leader" detail your mental challenges. How did you move from being the one doing all the work to the one assigning or leading in doing all the work?

4. What mistakes in leadership have you made lately? How did you recover from them? Why did you make the mistakes? How did your Jethro help you to see your mistake?

5. Look back over your life and identify three mentors who you admire. Now share what qualities they possessed that you admire. Do you have these qualities? Why or why not? Are you seeking ways to build these qualities within yourself?

Chapter 3

DEVELOPING RIGHT RELATIONSHIPS

One generation shall commend your works to another, and shall declare your mighty acts.

—Psalm 145:4

"A mentor is someone who allows you to see the hope inside yourself."

—Unknown

Developing the right relationships with correct boundaries in the body of Christ can take years. Sometimes it can take decades. However, for many of us life makes us feel as though we really don't have that much time. In this chapter, I would like to look at the mentor/ protégé relationship between two servant leaders. Some would call this a father/son relationship in the ministry, but for the purposes of this book we need to focus on the mentor/ protégé title. When we look at this relationship displayed throughout the Bible, we begin to see several areas that stand out which are listed below.

When a person enters into a mentor/protégé relationship there are four areas that both parties must learn to focus on. First, and probably the most important, they must build a lasting relationship with on-going communication. This walk on a journey filled with hills, valleys, and a few mountains for good measure to conquer all the obstacles life has placed in their pathway, both men need each other's support as they face their individual yet unique challenges. Second, they must learn to give advice without allowing their personal opinion to get hurt or damaged if the other party decides against their knowledge or wisdom. This speaks to the closeness of the bond they share. Sometimes, because of the nature of the relationship, there will be certain aspects of the mentor/ protégé relationship that's closer than a husband and wife. Third, they must understand that through their relationship they are to set an example in spiritual and world situations, meaning their decisions must always be about the best interest of the people and not their own personal desires. We must always keep in mind ministry is about the good of the people not the desires of the individual. When our personal desires begin to override our corporate mandate it's time for us to take a break to refocus on God. Fourth, they must understand that both parties will always need time and space to grow.

In our first chapter, we looked at the intricate relationship between Jethro and Moses. Yet, in this chapter, let's take a focused look and examine the relationship between Moses and Joshua. As the mentor/ protégé relationship carries a generational blessing (Enoch to Noah), let's take a look at the next generation after Jethro and Moses.

The relationship between Moses and Joshua is a peculiar one. In their core, they were drastically different, but both needed the strength of the other to accomplish their God-given tasks. Moses was the deliverer and Joshua the warrior, yet God bound both men together so they could fulfill their corporate and individual destinies.

It All Starts With Trust

The mentor/ protégé relationship must be an open and honest relationship in its foundation. If there is deceit and mistrust between the two parties then the model is broken. How can there be a true relationship if neither man would be open and honest to share his core thoughts, emotions, and issues in life or ministry?

Amos 3:3 addresses the heart of this question in the mentor/ protégé relationship when Amos writes "Can two walk together, unless they are agreed?"

I submit to you that trust is foundational for any relationship, but in the mentor/ protégé relationship it's an absolute necessity. If you can't trust the person you are currently walking with to look out for your best interests or to provide you sound wisdom why are you walking with him or her? If you can't talk to them about your struggles or issues in ministry why even begin the conversation? To walk in this Scripture means to "share a long journey with someone," and can you imagine sharing a long journey with someone you can't trust?

If you trust someone it means you will depend and rely on him or her in a time of need. Trust defined means you have an assured reliance on the character, ability, strength, or truth of someone or something. Now, does this sound like someone you want to be mentored by? Does this sound like the qualities that you seek in a mentor or a protégé?

When we begin to look into the life of Joshua we see his relationship with Moses took years to develop. Their time spent together teaches us a few lessons about the process of rearing true leaders. It takes time. Also, leaders are made; they're not born. Numbers 11:28 says, "Then Joshua the son of Nun, the attendant of Moses from his youth, said, 'Moses, my lord, restrain them.'"

The Bible does not detail everything about the life of Joshua. But here it teaches us that before the mantle of leadership was passed to Joshua he spent years of tutelage under the watchful eye of one of the greatest leaders in biblical times. In the beginning of their relationship, Joshua was not tasked with leading the people nor was he considered worthy of being the next military leader for the army of God. He was simply tasked with being Moses' servant.

Just because we see a person has the qualities of leadership that doesn't mean they're ready for leadership. Time and preparation are both key to the maturation process in developing leaders. Just because a person has potential that doesn't mean they're ready to carry the mantle.

During his years serving Moses, Joshua was privy to seeing Moses at the high points and low points of his personal and public life. He saw Moses at his strongest when he held out his staff over the Red Sea and the children of Israel walked over dry ground. He also saw Moses at his weakest when he allowed his frustration and emotions get the better of him as he struck the rock with his staff instead of speaking to it as God commanded and thereby excommunicating himself from the Promised Land.

Joshua was there through it all with Moses. He saw the good, bad, and ugly of leadership as he stood by his mentor's side.

This teaches us another vital point about the mentor/protégé relationship. The mentor must understand that the protégé is always watching to see how the mentor handles the issues of his life. In ministry, it's important for the protégé to hear how he needs to handle the storms of life, but it is also important for him to hear and see how you handle the storms in your life. This means often times the mentor will be spiritually exposed before the protégé. This is why the mentor must be prepared to lead by example.

I believe it's quite natural for leaders to desire to hide their scars from the church members or staff. However, in the mentor/ protégé relationship, I believe they should be put on display. Not in an act of self glorification or self righteousness, but in an effort to teach the next generation that by witnessing our sufferings it might help them to avoid some of their own. To do this causes the mentor to stand strong in faith because just as it is natural for us to hide our scars, it's also natural for the immature to misjudge our humility for weakness.

When a protégé sees his mentor going through trials and tribulations it often comes with an air of misunderstanding and judgment. This is why there needs to be complete open communication between the two parties. Oftentimes when the mentor is corrected by God or he makes a bad decision, the protégé, who's looking through immature eyes, judges the mentor harshly instead of with maturity and grace.

This is an attitude that many protégés carry until they are in the position of the mentor and have their own protégé looking over their shoulder.

I remember when I was a protégé looking over my mentor's shoulder I would often critique and criticize his decisions in my mind if things went wrong. Here's the funny thing though, I never critiqued or criticized him spiritually when he made the right decision. I would only do this when I perceived him making a mistake, and I walked with that mindset of judgmental superiority, that is, until I had my own protégé who critiqued and criticized my mistakes.

Although it wounded my spirit, I had to learn that this was also a part of the mentor/protégé relationship. My protégé had to see me fail and he needed to see how I handled that disappointment. I believe it was good for Joshua to see Moses' disappointment of not getting into the Promised Land. Maybe it helped him to make better decisions and become a better leader.

When we look into the life of Joshua not much is known of him before his ascendancy into power and purpose as Moses' armor bearer. Scripture lets us know that he performed a variety of tasks for Moses as he grew into church leadership and this must be recognized. Many people who want to be leaders will not suffer themselves to do the "little things." However, it is the willingness to do the little things that will show your mentor that you're ready for the bigger things of ministry.

The words of Christ echo this sentiment in Matthew 25:21 when He said, "You have been faithful with a few things; I will put you in charge of many things." In the area of leadership, there are many who want to be in-charge over the many things, but they have not proven themselves to be faithful over the few.

So how did Moses and Joshua begin their relationship? It started off small. As Moses groomed Joshua he began to rely on him more and more. This is not to say Moses didn't have other protégé's. Joshua just stood out from them all. If you look at Numbers 11:28, the text refers to Joshua as "one of his choice men." So the belief that Moses only mentored Joshua is false. I believe God allowed Moses and Joshua to see qualities in each other that they admired, and through the test and trials God placed in Moses' path Joshua began to separate himself from the group.

So how does a mentor determine the value of his protégé? He sifts them by examining their performance during their tasks and assignments.

First, the mentor must assign the protégé a task. Second, based on how the protégé approaches and completes his assignments, the mentor encourages, inspires, and sometimes, critiques their performance. Third, as those tasks and their completion become routine the mentor assigns additional tasks with increasing difficulty. As the protégé develops his management skills on a smaller scale the mentor slowly adds more and more responsibility so that the protégé, one day, will be able to manage his people and staff on a larger level.

As an example, when we first met Joshua he was considered a servant. However, as the years passed and their mentor/protégé relationship developed we begin to see Moses come to rely on Joshua more and more. We see this as Moses gave him jobs with increasing difficulty and importance. This is evident in Exodus 17:9 when Moses allowed Joshua to lead the army into battle for the first time. We must note that up until this time no other man was given this responsibility except Moses.

We will discuss this further along in the book, but for a protégé to grow in all areas the mentor must give them increasing power which means they must take a step back and share power.

It's All In How You Look At It

How you serve is all in how you look at it. Being a servant to a person can't be fun. "Go there! Do this! That's wrong! The page isn't centered. My water is too hot!" Ugh! Just thinking about someone barking orders at you can drive anybody to question being submissive to any form of a leader, let alone an obnoxious man or woman of God.

However, we need to remember that when we serve we are not serving people, we are serving God through people. Colossians 3:23-24 says, "And whatever you do, do it heartily, as to the Lord and not to men, knowing that from the Lord you will receive the reward of the inheritance; for you serve the Lord Christ."

In my tenure as a preacher of the Gospel, I had run into many petty men and women of God who think time stops when they walk into the room. The sad part about dealing with a ministry leader like this is, the same spirit they operate under usually flows down to their ministry teams.

Whenever I run into ministers of the Gospel with this type of attitude, I always try to look on the bright side of the ministry opportunity. Most times the only good thing was seeing them leave because I knew I would never invite them back.

So how do you serve bad leaders? Keep reminding yourself your service is unto the Lord. For all their negativity, I would not lose my connection with God by being angry and upset with the departing ministry.

Faithfulness is mandatory in developing strong leaders because faithfulness is a character trait. Faithfulness means being strict or thorough in the performance of duty or steady in allegiance or affection; loyal; constant. These are the traits that we must look for in the foundation of their character. These are the people who serve not for recognition or pay, but they serve because of their beliefs and their duty.

As Joshua served Moses he proved himself to be faithful in many areas. Joshua began as a servant (Numbers 11:28), became a warrior (Exodus 19:9-14), served as a spy (Numbers 13:16; 14:30, 38), and he was a minister (Exodus 32:17). Yet, in spite of all these job changes, he continued to transition and develop his leadership skills until he was announced by God as the successor to Moses to lead the Nation of Israel.

Ministry Succession: Your Choice or God's Choice

Now this is where many men of God make grievous mistakes. Oftentimes, they choose successors to follow them. From a review of the text, Moses for all his wisdom, did not attempt to choose his successor. He left that in God's capable hands.

This is a testament to the will and desire of Moses. Moses knew God was the only one who possessed the necessary insight to select the leader the people would need for the next leg of their journey into the Promised Land. So he prayed for someone who would follow the mission and desire God had for the people. Moses was not looking for someone to honor him. He was looking for someone to honor God.

Many leaders do not understand that leadership is fluid.

No man can control another leader's decisions and desires.

Let's look at the process of Moses transitioning out of leadership in Numbers 27:12-14. "Then the LORD said to Moses, 'Go up this mountain in the Abarim Range and see the land I have given the Israelites. After you have seen it, you too will be gathered to your people, as your brother Aaron was, for when the community rebelled at the waters in the Desert of Zin, both of you disobeyed my command to honor me as holy before their eyes.' (These were the waters of Meribah Kadesh, in the Desert of Zin.)"

This is a very important verse because it teaches us that God communicates to us that there comes a time when we all will need a successor. No man is meant to lead or live forever (although many tend to think so), and we must always be prepared for the transfer of succession in ministry as well as in the corporate world.

Also, God instructs Moses that it's time to get his affairs in order because death was approaching. Moses rises to the occasion and his reply demonstrates what a true leader looks like. Moses said, "May the LORD, the God who gives breath to all living things, appoint someone over this community to go out and come in before them, one who will lead them out and bring them in, so the Lord's people will not be like sheep without a shepherd."

Moses did not ask or request more time from God. He instantly began asking God to plant a strong successor to lead the people. In his position, Moses knew that the people would need a man who would lead them correctly and humbly before God. He knew they needed someone who would be an example to be followed. However, Moses did not seek a man like himself to succeed him, nor did he try to "pick" his successor. He knew that decision was not for him to make.

When a leader tries to choose his successor based on his own personal belief system, that's usually where the leadership model collapses.

As you read your Bible, you'll discover every time the Israelites tried to choose a leader or move ahead of God's pace for their lives they failed miserably. When they chose Saul for their leader it was a colossal failure. First Samuel 16 confirms that we have no idea how to choose a leader without God's assistance. Yes, the people chose out of their personal feelings when they chose Saul. We understand they saw him as a tall, good looking man, and although Samuel warned them of the things Saul would do when he became king, they persisted in their desire and it brought shame to the nation.

Even Samuel made the same mistake as the people of God did when he was sent to Jesse's house. He looked on the outside and he allowed his eyes to select a king without talking to God. First Samuel 16:6 teaches us as soon as the eldest son Eliab walked into the room Samuel declared him the king in his own spirit. The Scripture says, "Surely the Lord's anointed is before Him!" And this is our downfall. We try to confirm externally what we felt internally, and that's not the way God wants us to operate.

In Samuel's mind, he was already anointing Eliab as the next king based upon how he looked and not who he was. This is the same sin that the people committed when they selected Saul. As leaders we must remember even fake gold glitters.

When God spoke to Samuel about Eliad, he let him know that leadership selection can only be determined by God because He is the only One who can truly see what lies in the heart of man. God said, "Do not look at his appearance or at his physical stature, because I have refused him. For the Lord does not see as man sees; for man looks at the outward appearance, but the Lord looks at the heart."

When I think of this Scripture I have to chuckle because after Eliab, Jesse made all the sons he considered worthy to walk before Samuel one by one. As each hopeful, yet denied candidate passed before Samuel, I am sure he began to become nervous because we often think having someone in place is better than not having anyone at all. But that is our flesh talking. As leaders, we must learn to remain silent as Samuel did when potential replacements pass by, and wait for God to confirm who will be the next successor.

Can you imagine that the king God chose is the one son Jesse failed to consider? This is why we can't choose our successor. It's usually the one we never consider who turns out to be God's first choice.

Over my years in ministry I have often witnessed pastors selecting their paternal sons to be their successor and soon, thereafter, the wheels just fall off. I've seen God allow these great men of God to build healthy churches, and instead of allowing God to choose their successor they select their "chosen one" and within two years it all comes crashing down.

The danger in a pastor selecting his son to follow him in ministry is closely aligned to the story of the prodigal son. While the father worked tirelessly to build a great environment to support his two sons, one son learned the cost of keeping the farm because he worked for the father. However, the prodigal son wasted his inheritance because he never learned to work for what he was given.

So when that pastor or business owner who worked for years hands over all his hard labor to the son he loves but who never learned the ministry or the business and the son destroys the church, can we really be surprised?

Once Moses entreated God and asked who would be his successor God confirmed His choice. So the LORD said to Moses, "Take Joshua son of Nun, a man in whom is the spirit of leadership, and lay your hand on him." This is the private ceremony of the transfer of leadership. Biblically, the transfer of leadership is done with the "laying of hands." Symbolically, it means that power is about to be transferred from one person to another. Paul spoke about this in the New Testament when he told the leaders to stop laying hands on people so quickly because they did not know the type of spirit that was in these men. First Timothy 5:21-22 says, "I charge you before God and the Lord Jesus Christ and the elect angels that you observe these things without prejudice, doing nothing with partiality. Do not lay hands on anyone hastily, nor share in other people's sins; keep yourself pure."

Many of us go through this type of ceremony whenever we ascend to a higher position on the job or in the church. Our superiors will often pull us aside and give us our new duties, and they often come with a "come to Jesus meeting" which is a conversation that alludes to us understanding that with new responsibilities come new duties, new trials, and new temptations.

I have come to believe that in every ministry there can be no success without a successor. This is shown more in the church that anywhere else in society. As the Bible teaches us, when there is no pastor to lead the people, they will scatter like sheep without a shepherd. It is impossible for sheep to shepherd sheep. If a leader dies or is voted out without a successor, that church usually falls into utter chaos. This is the time that insecure or vain personalities rise up and begin fighting over the church which leads the church down a dark bottomless pit.

Many times these men who "think they are doing God's work" are actually operating in the spirit of Korah.

When we look at the rebellion of Korah, we see that it's no more than vanity and pride run amok. It is a jealous spirit that seeks to raise itself up and destroy good leadership. "Now Korah the son of Izhar, the son of Kohath, the son of Levi, with Dathan and Abiram the sons of Eliab, and On the son of Peleth, sons of Reuben, took men; and they rose up before Moses with some of the children of Israel, two hundred and fifty leaders of the congregation, representatives of the congregation, men of renown. They gathered together against Moses and Aaron, and said to them, 'You take too much upon yourselves, for all the congregation is holy, every one of them, and the Lord is among them. Why then do you exalt yourselves above the assembly of the Lord?'"

The first thing we need to understand about Korah is he has leadership skills. If he didn't how could he persuade 250 men to follow him to his doom? Korah was a man that "if" he had allowed God to use his talents for helping the people he would have been a tremendous blessing for the Israelites. Instead, he allowed his pride to turn him away from being a blessing to the people to being a stumbling block for the people. The Bible teaches us that he was persuasive and he led the people into open rebellion against God and His established order.

The text says "they rose up before Moses with some of the children of Israel, two hundred and fifty leaders of the congregation, representatives of the congregation, men of renown." This is the spirit of rebellion, and it lives in many of our churches, families, and ministries. I can't count how many times I have counseled pastors who are constantly being fought tooth and nail by their deacons or trustees ministry over who holds Godly authority in the church. In the church, the spirit of Korah runs rampant in these two groups. In the boardroom, this spirit usually inhabits those who are directly under the decision makers in the company.

Please note this "rebellion" isn't led by the church members or the people. This spirit hovers in the second tier of leadership in the church or corporation thinking that they have the same anointing as the first.

Like Korah, many think since God can speak to us all then we do not have to truly submit to the leadership. But they miss that our God is a God of order. They must realize that people who usurp power and authority through illicit gains will not succeed in spiritual matters. The text teaches us that Korah developed a large following based on deceptive means. He had many leaders coming on board with his message of false leadership and it was simply a power play. Korah wanted to be equal with Moses in position and authority, but in the end it cost him dearly.

However, when it comes to Christian authority and church operation God still has an order when it comes to the church.

Keep in mind Korah was a Levite and a first cousin to Moses. This means he was a man who took care of the tabernacle of God, and he was a man who was constantly around the holy things of God. When we are surrounded by the vessels of God we admire their beauty, and many become jealous of the man who God places the mantle of leadership upon. Instead of Korah being happy in his position, he desired and craved Moses' position of power, so he devised a plan to unseat him.

Some people are only momentarily happy in their service to God. They are happy with their gift, but when they see someone who has more gifts they immediately become jealous and envious. I heard Dr. Samuel J. Gilbert say, "If you got one gift be thankful! Because you only have to give God an account for one."

As I mentioned earlier in this chapter, when a mentor goes through the trials of life, oftentimes their protégés are witness to their issues and struggles. With Korah being a Levite, it is natural to assume that he witnessed a lot of the challenges that Moses had to face as did Joshua. But instead of him praying for and covering his pastor, he decided to attack and sought to minimize him in front of the congregation.

I must applaud Moses for he truly possessed refined leadership skills. Although he was challenged, belittled, and made to feel small, he still tried to reason with Korah before God pronounced judgment on him and his family. This is what a true leader should do when attacked. He should try to bring peace between himself and his brother.

Moses never considered stepping down or letting Korah have his way as many leaders do today. That was never in question. However, Moses did try to explain to Korah that he was already in a blessed position, but his words simply rained on blocked ears.

In his pursuit of promotion, Korah forgot the blessing of being #2 in ministry, and he was lost in his desire to be #1. In his pursuit of establishing his own priesthood, Korah forgot God was the one who established Moses. So by challenging Moses he was really fighting God.

Do you think God liked Korah challenging and despising His established order? Absolutely not! When you read the text you can see God's attitude towards Korah's rebellion. When God responded, He did not dilly-dally nor did He speak wonderful and glorious revelation to the people. God said, " Moses, you better get out of the way because I am going to kill them!" Not that I am trying to embellish God's words, but He said, "Separate yourselves from among this congregation, that I may consume them in a moment."

So what's God's attitude towards His children who allow jealousy to be their guide as they seek to challenge His ordained leaders? Destruction.

Because of his sin, Korah, his family, and the people who followed him came to a disastrous end. The Bible teaches us that God performed a "new thing" in the destruction of Korah and these men. "And Moses said: 'By this you shall know that the LORD has sent me to do all these works, for I have not done them of my own will. If these men die naturally like all men, or if they are visited by the common fate of all men, then the LORD has not sent me. But if the LORD creates a new thing, and the earth opens its mouth and swallows them up with all that belongs to them, and they go down alive into the pit, then you will understand that these men have rejected the LORD.' Now it came to pass, as he finished speaking all these words, that the ground split apart under them, and the earth opened its mouth and swallowed them up, with their households and all the men with Korah, with all their goods. So they and all those with them went down alive into the pit; the earth closed over them, and they perished from among the assembly. Then all Israel who were around them fled at their cry, for they said, 'Lest the earth swallow us up also!'"

What's Private Should Be Made Public

In Numbers 27:19-21, we see Joshua's public ceremony. We see the coronation of the new leader in the sight of Moses and the people of God. This public display of commissioning Joshua does several things. It supplants any man's thought of taking power and raising himself up as David's son Adonijah tried to do before his death. The Bible teaches us David almost died without announcing a successor, so Adonijah placed himself as king since he was the oldest and many people followed him. In this instance, David's hesitancy of announcing a successor almost cost Solomon the kingdom (1st Kings 1:5-6).

When you take a deep look at Adonijah you see he had three things going for him. He had an old father who was barely coherent, he was the oldest living heir so according to the law he was next in line to be king, and he was a good looking man. In the mindset of the people, he would have been the next logical choice. However, the logical choice doesn't always add up to be the Godly choice. Plus, as David lay on his deathbed, Adonijah thought he could do whatever he wanted and not worry about repercussion from David.

So Adonijah "exalted himself." This is bad leadership:101. Never toot your own horn. It is reminiscent of another one who tooted his horn and he had a biblical name change. The Bible teaches us that Lucifer (Light Bringer) was a chief Cherub (Angel), but he was blinded by his beauty and he issued several statements that showed his true heart before God (Isaiah 14:12-15).

The five "I Will's" of Satan reminds us of the one "I will" of Adonijah when he said, "I will be king."

Jealousy and lust for power have derailed many men on the way to their purpose and destiny. Instead of seeing positions of power as honorable pursuit, they see them as a personal conquest usually to the detriment of those in society.

Man's lust for spiritual power can never be fulfilled by the fleshly pursuits. This is why God wouldn't allow Adonijah's nor Korah's rebellion to go forward. Each man, in his own way, did not challenge the human leader but the One who put that leader in place which is God Himself. In their haste to destroy their Moses and Solomon, it inevitably backfired costing them their lives.

In both situations, the mantle of leadership was passed according to God's plan to the next successor. Moses passed his mantle to Joshua. David passed his mantle to Solomon. Both men endured a private coronation and a public coronation before the people of God which confirmed God's hand on both their lives.

Study Guide

Chapter 3: Developing Right Relationships

1. Get a sheet of paper and begin to write down all the people in your life who you think are mentors. Write down the reason you trust them and ask yourself do you believe they can trust you. Write down the qualities in them you admire and look within yourself and see if you possess those same characteristics. Why or why not?

2. Have you discussed your "scars" with your mentor or protégé? Why or why not?

3. How do you look at your ministry? Do you look at it as if you are serving God, or are you serving man? Identify someone you admire and see how they operate in ministry or in their job duties. Do they enjoy what they do? Do they inspire you to be the best you can be? What attributes do they have that you can identify with? Do you have the same spirit of excellence in your duties as they have in their profession? If not, explain.

4. When it comes to selection and promotion are you praying for God to send you a worthy replacement? Or have you hand- picked your successor? If you picked them for your own personal reasons how can God have a say in whom He wants to succeed you?

5. Have you seen any men or women operating in the spirit of Korah? What does it mean to you that in his pursuit of being Moses' equal it cost him his ministry and his life? What area of pride do you have in your ministry, on your job, or at church?

Chapter 4

MANAGING YOUR TRANSITIONS

"Do not be conformed to this world, but be transformed by the renewing of your mind, that you may prove what is that good and acceptable and perfect will of God."

—Romans 12:2

"In learning you will teach, and in teaching you will learn."

—Phil Collins

For the next few pages I would like to share with you how to manage your transitions in mentor/ protégé relationship. To fully understand this, we must discuss the differences between change and transition in the mentor/ protégé model.

From the outset of their relationship Moses and Joshua endured three transitions. Their first transition was growing closer together as mentor and protégé. Their second transition was them fulfilling their individual and collective destinies. Their third transition was their ascensions from level to level in God.

For a brief moment let's look at the life of Christ, and let's begin discussing change vs. transition. So, does God change? Well, according to Malachi

3:6, the answer is no. The text says, "For I am the Lord, I do not change; Therefore you are not consumed, O sons of Jacob."

When we take a look at the life of Christ we see from His birth He was All-God and All-Man. When he grew up as a tender shoot before God (Isaiah 53:2) until His awful death on an old rugged cross He was All-God and All-Man. During His entire earthly life His collective nature of being All-God and All-Man never changed; however, He did have to transition.

During this time of transitional growth His body and mind developed as well as His spirit. He transitioned from a babe to a child, from a child to a boy, from a boy to a man, and from a man to the Savior of the world. So it does not matter what situation He faced during the humanly portion of His life; He was still the Savior of the World and He did not change. He simply transitioned.

Understanding Change vs Transition

Now, before I confuse you, let's discuss the differences between change and transition. To change means to be placed in a completely new situation or environment. To transition means how I progress from point A to point B as I travel along my past heading to my destiny.

Understand that change is an external phenomenon. Transitioning is an internal phenomenon.

Change has to do with the situation you find yourself in. Transitioning has to deal with how you process your internal challenges to cope with your external situation. When we look at the forty-two steps from Glory to Glory of Christ we notice He never changed, but He transitioned with every step.

Here's an example. When the Children of Israel left Egypt they changed their (physical) location but they did not change their (mental) processes. When God sent them out of Egypt He gave them the wealth of Egypt, but they still maintained their slave mentality. See, God changed their external location, but their minds never transitioned along with the change.

This is why when things became rough for them as they walked to the Promised Land they would continually beg to go back to Egypt and the abuses of Pharaoh. Can you imagine a freed people who were abused for over 400 years by tyrants begging to come back under the lash of their whip because they were hungry and thirsty? This doesn't even sound rational, does it?

When God calls us to Himself He calls us to salvation (Romans 10:9-10). Once saved the goal of God is to transition us from being children of wrath to being children of the Light (Ephesians 2:1-6). God does this by transitioning our minds through our daily walk (Romans 12:2).

So understand when Christ saved you, He changed your spiritual location from being dead in sin to being alive in Christ. Hallelujah!

But, now that you are saved, it is incumbent that you allow God to begin transitioning your thinking so that you can deal with the changes and challenges that life will present to you. How do we start the process of transitioning our minds? It starts by studying the Word of God and allowing it to change our thinking (2nd Timothy 2:15). When we do this we begin transitioning our minds, and eventually, our living will follow suit as we seek to please God.

When we accept salvation from God but don't read His Word, we're like the Israelites. We have been given freedom, but we still walk in spiritual bondage.

Why am I striving to show the difference between change and transition? As children of God we must transition (internally) before people see the change (externally). In today's world, too many so called Christians seek to show Christ (externally), but they have never transitioned (internally). So, in essence, they are living a lie.

A perfect example of this lie is the fig tree that looked like it had figs. The text lets us know it wasn't the season for figs but since it looked like it had fruit Christ inspected it. When He didn't find any figs on it, He cursed it. With this as our example, what will Christ do when He comes back and inspects our lives? Will He curse us because we look as if we have fruit to displace externally but we never possess fruit internally? Change and transitioning both focus on the outcome. Another difference between the two is change is only just concerned with the finished product and transitioning adopts a step by step approach to move from where you are presently to your planned goal.

People who view life through the "change" perspective will preach "you must be perfect 24/7". They will preach a legalistic gospel that doesn't give the believer any room for grace or mercy. The reason they do this is because they have "changed," and once you've changed then there are no excuses. It must be done perfectly every time.

However, a person who transitions assumes a " we personality" because that person understands the struggle. People who view life through a " transition" perspective will preach "growing in God is a process."

As Christ transitioned so we will have to transition. Christ transitioned step by step in His forty-two steps from Glory to Glory, and so will we. Look at the Christian journey as a marathon that will last a lifetime rather than a sprint to a goal.

As they (leaders) transition they know that sometimes in ministry they will be hurt by their brothers and sisters who are transitioning as well. They know that in relationship there will be good days and bad days, and they understand on this journey there will be wins and losses. They also understand the process of letting go as God elevates them.

Let's say an unsaved person who has never met a Christian comes to church one day and the pastor preaches so well that person comes to salvation. Later that day, he meets the pastor and he says, "Okay, what are you going to change about your life?"

Well, since this person hasn't read his Bible he doesn't know what he needs to change or how to change. What about the other issues of life? What about his damaged family relationships? What does she do with the live-in boyfriend? What is tithing? What does he or she do with his or her kid who is selling drugs out of his or her house?

Now, do you think a person can deal with all this on day one? I don't think so. I believe it takes awhile. As we transition through life and we learn more and more about God, we begin to see things His way and we pull all these things down to obedience to Him.

Room For Growth

With all the changes and transitions in ministry room for growth is mandatory. As the relationship for mentor/ protégé begins we must understand it will end in God's time and at the destination God selects. However, three things are mandatory for the mentor. First, he must teach his protégé everything God has instructed him. Second, he must be willing to transition out of ministry as his mentor supersedes him. Third, he must understand sometimes his mentorship is for a season, sometimes for a lifetime.

When we are first introduced to Joshua we see that Joshua was Moses' assistant. However, over the course of their relationship, we see both men transitioning through the encounters they faced together and as individuals. Early on in his ministry, Joshua made a mistake interpreting the will of God. But, instead of ridiculing him, Moses corrected him in love the same way Jethro corrected him when he judged the people by himself.

In Numbers 11, God had come down and He had taken the spirit of Moses and placed the same spirit on the seventy elders who stood before the Tent of the Meeting. But in Numbers 11:26- 28, Joshua made a mistake interpreting the power of God. The text says, "But two men had remained in the camp: the name of one was Eldad, and the name of the other Medad. And the Spirit rested upon them. Now they were among those listed, but who had not gone out to the tabernacle; yet they prophesied in the camp. And a young man ran and told Moses, and said, 'Eldad and Medad are prophesying in the camp.' So Joshua the son of Nun, Moses' assistant, one of his choice men, answered and said, 'Moses my lord, forbid them!'"

As a mentor transitions throughout the ministry, it is mandatory he teaches his subordinates how to see in the Spirit. This was the issue Elisha had with his servant (II Kings 6:15-17). Ministry is hard work. While God was performing this miracle Joshua did not understand the weight that was on Moses' shoulders. The two men who he would have stopped from prophesying were prophesying under the anointing of God. Yes, the text says these men were on the list to be at the meeting of this spiritual transference but for whatever reason they did not come. However, this did not stop God from touching, anointing, and using them.

You can run but you can't hide! If God wants to touch, anoint, and use you it does not matter where you run to. If God can find Jonah He can find you too!

When Moses heard the voice of Joshua, he said as is recorded in Numbers 11:29: "Then Moses said, 'Are you zealous for my sake? Oh, that all the LORD's people were prophets and that the LORD would put His Spirit upon them!' And Moses returned to the camp, he and the elders of Israel." Moses' question was one to remind Joshua that this is God's work. The only way the Spirit could fall on them would be if God would send the Spirit to them. Right? So this was the Lawd's Work!

Yes, if it was out of concern for Moses I am sure he would have appreciated it. No pastor wants to carry the entire burden of leading the people of God. Moses had to lead over four million people, so he knew the rigors of ministry and He did not want individual power. He wanted shared power.

Remember, Moses was a "doer" initially, but He was trained to be a "leader." Also remember that shared power is the best form of power in the church or corporate world because it gets everyone involved in the tasks of the organization.

The next time we see Joshua we see him in a totally different capacity. In our first view, we saw him as a servant. In the second situation, we saw him as an inexperienced judgmental leader. However, in the third text, we see him as a military leader. In Exodus 17:8-10, the text says, "Now Amalek came and fought with Israel in Rephidim. And Moses said to Joshua, 'Choose us some men and go out, fight with Amalek. Tomorrow I will stand on the top of the hill with the rod of God in my hand.' So Joshua did as Moses said to him, and fought with Amalek."

This is our first showing of both men operating in ministry together as mentor and protégé. Both men were servant leaders, but God used them to perform their own specific duties. Moses was leading and entreating God for the people, and Joshua was leading and fighting for the people.

Did you see that? Both men were leading in their specific areas. One was praying and the other was fighting, but both were in the leadership roles in their respective areas.

Now talk about a transition! From servant to military leader. But God has another transition for Moses and Joshua to go through. In Exodus 24:13-14, Joshua is invited into the presence of God. Mentors, the ultimate goal of your ministry is to introduce your protégé to the God you serve. The text says, "Then the LORD said to Moses, 'Come up to Me on the mountain and be there; and I will give you tablets of stone, and the law and commandments which I have written, that you may teach them.' So Moses arose with his assistant Joshua, and Moses went up to the mountain of God. And he said to the elders, 'Wait here for us until we come back to you. Indeed, Aaron and Hur are with you. If any man has a difficulty, let him go to them.' Then Moses went up into the mountain, and a cloud covered the mountain."

Notice, Moses didn't ask Joshua if he wanted to come up on the mountain to meet God. Moses took him. Mentors, sometimes for our protégés to understand what God has for them we must put them in place to experience God instead of trying to tell them about God.

If you look in Exodus 33:7-11, you will see a marvelous sight. The text says after the people sinned by worshipping the golden calf that "Moses took his tent and pitched it outside the camp, far from the camp, and called it the tabernacle of meeting.

And it came to pass that everyone who sought the Lord went out to the tabernacle of meeting which was outside the camp. So it was, whenever Moses went out to the tabernacle, that all the people rose, and each man stood at his tent door and watched Moses until he had gone into the tabernacle. And it came to pass, when Moses entered the tabernacle that the pillar of cloud descended and stood at the door of the tabernacle, and the Lord talked with Moses. All the people saw the pillar of cloud standing at the tabernacle door, and all the people rose and worshiped, each man in his tent door. So the Lord spoke to Moses face to face, as a man speaks to his friend. And he would return to the camp, but his servant Joshua the son of Nun, a young man, did not depart from the tabernacle."

The Bible teaches us that Moses spoke to God "face to face as to a friend." However, when Moses had to leave the tabernacle, Joshua was there to oversee and protect the camp. Notice the text says, "Joshua the son of Nun, a young man, did not depart from the tabernacle."

I believe Moses and God became comfortable enough with Joshua that they deemed it necessary for him to stay at the Tabernacle of the Meeting when Moses would go into the tribes to visit the people of God.

The final transition of the great mentor/ protégé relationship happened when God called Moses home to Glory. These words are confirmed by God in the book of Joshua chapter 1:1-2 where it says, "After the death of Moses the servant of the Lord, it came to pass that the Lord spoke to Joshua the son of Nun, Moses' assistant, saying: 'Moses My servant is dead.'"

Everything that has a beginning must have an end.

In our life, we move through seasons and this is also true for relationships. When it comes to relationship we generally have four "seasons" and they are beginning, continuation, decline, and end. Here in this text, we see that Moses and Joshua mentor/ protégé relationship had concluded with the death of Moses on Mount Nebo. Although Moses had poured all his knowledge into Joshua, there were still many things about God that Joshua needed to learn, and the first thing was how to entreat God himself.

When we look back on the life of Moses, we see that Moses met God because of a burning bush on the side of the Mount, and God spoke to Moses from the bush. However, when God showed Himself He did not use a bush. He showed Himself as a warrior. As Moses was a shepherd, it would be natural for him to looked for shaded areas in the desert so he might find rest for himself and his flock. As Joshua was a warrior, it was quite natural for him to look at another warrior and see certain characteristics and traits that he valued himself.

Show Time-Visions and Dreams

Visions and dreams validate the call of God as we move throughout the ministry. Let's look at the text in Joshua chapter 5:13-15. "And it came to pass, when Joshua was by Jericho, that he lifted his eyes and looked, and behold, a Man stood opposite him with His sword drawn in His hand. And Joshua went to Him and said to Him, 'Are You for us or for our adversaries?' So He said, 'No, but as Commander of the army of the LORD I have now come.' And Joshua fell on his face to the earth and worshiped, and said to Him, 'What does my Lord say to His servant?' Then the Commander of the LORD's army said to Joshua, 'Take your sandal off your foot, for the place where you stand is holy.' And Joshua did so."

God showed Himself to Moses and Joshua in a way that not only confirmed their destiny but encouraged their hearts!

Notice that when God showed Himself to Joshua it was during a stressful time for Joshua. Moses was dead, the people looked to him for leadership, the fighting men were sore from being circumcised, and now they were on the eve of their first battle. So,saying that Joshua was under extreme pressure might be putting it lightly. But notice that God did not forsake Joshua. Thank God our Father never leaves us during our stressful times.

Notice as Joshua goes for this evening walk to clear his head that God shows Himself to Joshua but Joshua did not recognize the Lord. The text says, ". . . a Man stood opposite him with His sword drawn in His hand. And Joshua went to Him and said to Him, 'Are You for us or for our adversaries?'" Many of us must be taught to see God in our lives. Many of us walk blindly through our day by day existence and we never look to see God's hands moving in our lives.

I remember my first vision of God as if it was yesterday. I remember our conversation and I remember the smells of the apple orchard He and I were standing in. I hold on to that vision today. When God brought me into the vision I didn't ask who He was; my spirit confirmed who He was before the conversation began.

In answer to His question if he was for the Israelites or not, God said, "No, but as Commander of the army of the LORD I have now come." And Joshua fell on his face to the earth and worshiped, and said to Him, "What does my Lord say to His servant?" Brothers and sisters, it's not for God to get on our page; it's for us to get on His page. He is the ruler of the world, and when God shares with Joshua who He really is Joshua realizes he is in the presence of the Divine.

The thing that I love about the conclusion of this chapter has to deal with that of being submissive. He begins asking God for orders.

Before God will tell you what to do, He will tell you how to act in His presence.

What is it about us that looks to "do something" for God instead of just resting in His presence? He is divine and this was the first time that Joshua "saw" God. But it was a vision that would carry him the rest of his life. I believe this vision should have been shared with the next generation, but we will discover in the next chapter that moments like this should be eternally shared with those who seek to learn more about God. This way, they will learn the history and the mighty miracles of the God we serve, instead of falling away into the seduction of the world we live in.

Study Guide

Chapter 4: Managing Your Transitions

1. Get a mirror and look deeply at the face you see. Over your life have you changed your face? Your eyes? Or lips? Or have you kept the same facial features but you have transitioned with age? Is there beauty in what you see? Compare this with the knowledge that you are spiritually transitioning. God takes the spiritual features that you were born with and He uses them to be a blessing to this world. Now is there beauty in what you see?

2. Can you write down three things that you have spiritually transitioned towards or away from?

3. Think back when you were a protégé. Can you see things in your current leadership style that remind you of your mentor? Can you see anything that you do similar to those who mentored you? If not, explain.

4. How many transitions have you gone through in your life?

5. When God transitions you how has He shown Himself to you?

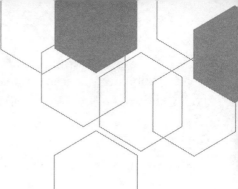

Chapter 5

THE DROPPED BATON

"When all that generation had been gathered to their fathers, another generation arose after them who did not know the LORD nor the work which He had done for Israel."

—Judges 2:10

"I can accept failure, but I can't accept not trying."

—Unknown

For the next few pages I would like to concentrate on what I feel is the saddest day in the history of the Israelites as it pertains to the mentor/protégé relationship. The text for this travesty in history can be found in one Scripture. In Judges 2:10 it reads, "When all that generation had been gathered to their fathers, another generation arose after them who did not know the LORD nor the work which He had done for Israel."

How do we lose an entire generation? How do we miss training our next generation of leaders?

If you look at Christian leadership through the eyes of ministry succession, you will see that it is a chain that should never be broken. Every father (or leader) raises a son. When that son matures he becomes a father who raises a son to take his place and so on. As one generation retires to their reward, there should always be a new generation ready to carry on with the work of

Christ. With this type of structure in place, there should never been a time in our history when we have a generation that has no idea who Jehovah is.

However, one generation after the Israelites entered the Promised Land that is exactly what happened. Somehow, an entire generation lost their connection with the Lord of hosts. As the children of God moved into their Promised Land, they carried with them two assurances. One, God was going to instruct them in how they should subdue the land; and two, they would have to fight for every victory.

Knowing they would have to stay close to God and keep fighting the "good fight" should have kept them focused on the prize. Be that as it may, soon the Israelites began to do something we typically do when things are going our way. They became complacent and they neglected their duties toward God and each other. Then they began the slow descent from being the "righteousness of God" to the "so-so" of God.

My Actions (and My Non-Actions) Cause Reactions

When the children of Israel came into the Promised Land the rules were simple. Kill everything. This was the plan of God from the very beginning. However, the Israelites allowed their slave mentality to creep back in and slowly they began to intermingle with the tribes that were still in the land.

If one were to ask why God wanted the Israelites to kill everything in the land, the answer is, the Israelites were young in their faith and they were easily influenced. If you have two spirits in one house, the stronger spirit will always rule the weaker. These Israelites were young in faith compared to the Canaanites that dwelt in the land, so they were easily influenced by their teachings, customs, and ways.

God had called the Israelites to live differently and worship the one true God. The Canaanites believed in worshipping multiple gods, just like the Egyptians. So, here we have catastrophe waiting to happen. Although God had brought the Israelites out of Egypt, it took less than fifty years for them to corrupt their destiny by attaching themselves to people exactly like their former masters.

Proverbs 26:11 says, "As a dog returns to his own vomit, so a fool repeats his folly." Do you see the Israelites returning to their folly? Do you see them returning to their old ways?

When we decide we are strong enough to handle it, we tend to get ourselves into more trouble than it's worth.

God's instructions to the Israelites were simple. In Deuteronomy 18:9-13, God said, "When you come into the land which the LORD your God is giving you, you shall not learn to follow the abominations of those nations. There shall not be found among you anyone who makes his son or his daughter pass through the fire, or one who practices witchcraft, or a soothsayer, or one who interprets omens, or a sorcerer, or one who conjures spells, or a medium, or a spiritist, or one who calls up the dead. For all who do these things are an abomination to the LORD, and because of these abominations the LORD your God drives them out from before you. You shall be blameless before the LORD your God."

This list provides us with a "who's who" list of demonic activity and satanic worship that was found inside the Promised Land. This is why God did not want them to affiliate with the people of the land as they would turn their hearts from God.

Now do you understand why God wanted them to kill everything they encountered?

God wanted His children blameless, and He knew if left unchecked these people would contaminate their hearts and minds with their demonic worship.

God has called us to walk worthy before Him, and we can't be blameless when we're involved in sin and witchcraft. I believe this is Satan's way of contaminating us, and that is the way he inspired Balaam to trap the Israelites into sin. Spiritual contamination doesn't start in your actions; it starts in your thinking. This is why Proverbs 23:7 says, "As a man thinks in his heart, so is he."

If you don't know it by now, the devil has plans for you. Sure, God has plans, but the enemy of the world has plans as well. Ephesians 6:11 says, "Put on the whole armor of God that you may be able to stand against the wiles of the devil."

So what are the wiles of the devil? If you translate the meaning of the word "wiles" it means "methods". By definition, a method is a procedure, technique, or way of doing something, especially in accordance with a definite plan.

With this in mind, we should know that the enemy wants to trip us up. So what are some of the methods that he has used to attach, discourage, confuse, or accuse you? However he approaches you, it will come from three areas of lust. He will appeal to the lust of the flesh, the lust of the eyes, or the pride of life. But for this to work, the first thing he has to do is make you numb.

Have you ever had to go under the knife for surgery? If you have, then you know about anesthesia. Anesthesia is the condition of having your senses blocked. For instance, when you are feeling fine and nothing is hurting, there is no reason for anesthesia. However, if you have to have surgery, it means your body will be in a lot of pain, so to keep you from suffering, the doctor will put you under anesthesia and make you numb to the surgery.

This is how the devil desires us to feel: Numb to the things of God. He desires us to grow cold toward God so we can't feel His presence or discern His will in our lives.

Over the past twenty years, I've had four surgeries and I always hated going under anesthesia. During the surgery process, I know anesthesia is mandatory, but the immediate sensation always left me feeling sick and nauseous. Over time, I noticed it didn't matter if I was given the medicine through an IV or if I had to breathe it in through my nostrils. In either case , the immediate impact of the medicine left me feeling cold and discombobulated.

Maybe his (Satan's) plan is to contaminate you by provoking you to cheat on your wife. Maybe his plans are to cause you to start drinking again. Who knows how he will try to make you stumble and fall. Rest assured he is going to try something!

No Succession

Jethro mentored Moses. Moses mentored Joshua. But who did Joshua mentor? In Joshua 24, we see Joshua has called all the tribes and their leaders to reconfirm their covenant to God and there seems to be one person missing—Joshua's protégé.

I have long believed there can be no succession without a successor. When we looked into the life of Jethro we see Moses, and when we look into the life of Moses we see Joshua, but there is no one after Joshua. Do you think Joshua thought he would live forever?

Although this is a very sad text, it is still a very true text in the lives of many church leaders. Pastors who have a "doer" mentality simply focus on day to day operations, hoping and praying they never get too old to complete their duties. So that begs the question: How old is too old? Sure, the pastor might be able to stand for twenty minutes, but if you can't preach a sound, substantive, theologically correct passage, it is time for you to resign.

In my previous book, *Everybody Can't Climb This Mountain*, I spoke about my first pastorate and replacing one of the first pastors who watched over my soul. When I was first alerted about the position, I knew Pastor Richards had been the pastor of Shiloh for over thirty years. However, that isn't his whole story because Pastor Richards was first called as a deacon for twenty years before becoming a minister for ten years, and then the pastor of Shiloh for thirty years. So he was faithful for a long time.

Time and old age began creeping in on Pastor Richards and a replacement became necessary. There was a time when Pastor Richards could quote the Bible, but, in his final years, his ability to preach was gone. His body had broken down to the point where he could not walk and all he could say was "Praise the Lord, baby!" When the body of believers began seeing this, they tried to aid the ministry by bringing in young ministers to assist him. This effort failed miserably as the young ministers began stealing money from the church.

Being this was my home community, I soon received a phone call and began researching to see if there was any way I could help the church. After seeing Pastor Richards one Sunday, I was asked if I would like to become the church's assistant pastor. When I met with the leadership, I told them I could not take that position because they needed a pastor not an assistant. I went on to share with them that my thoughts were not aggressive or self-serving but that time catches up with us all, and once our "time of ministry" has passed, it is time for us to relinquish the position of pastor in the church.

Allowing him to stay in the pastoral position actually wounded the sheep. No man can preach, teach, or guide the church forever. We all have a date in our future when we need to resign the position of pastor.

The problem that many of us have is, we confuse our call to minister with our role as pastor. When a man or woman is called by God, he or she is called to the five-fold ministry and this is a lifelong office. However, there are some offices that aren't life- long because they are positions that are purpose oriented. For instance, the term pastor, overseer, or bishop speaks to an office and not a calling. Sure, in today's world, we use the terms interchangeably. But by the letter , they must be separated.

Let's dissect this issue. When I was called by God to become a preacher a month after my twenty-fifth birthday, I began walking in my calling. Before I was licensed by the church, I was a minister of God because of the calling He placed on my life. Sure, I didn't know my role or responsibilities but that is secondary. From the moment God spoke to me in my dorm room, I was confirmed as a minister of the Gospel.

Over the years, I have worn many different titles depending on what church function I attended. I have been called Preacher, Elder, Reverend, or Doctor; but at the end of the day these titles mean little because my role has not changed. I am still a minister of the Gospel of Jesus Christ.

Even today I serve in the position of pastor, but that doesn't change my role. I am still a minister of God. This is the thing about operating in a role. Just as they are given, they can be taken away.

In twenty years, if God says the same, I plan to step back from the Senior Pastor position and pour into the younger preachers' lives who God has working in the temple He has assigned me to. Notice, I did not say I would stop being a minister of the Gospel. That is something I can never walk away from. But one day, either due to time, my health failing, or my completion of twenty-five years in the senior pastor position, I plan to retire from the position and spend the rest of my days traveling with my wife and enjoying the rest of our lives together.

Now I have shared with you a small portion of how I came to pastor my first church. Please allow me to share with you how God called me to resign from my position.

In late 2009, God began stirring my spirit to start praying for a successor. Later, God began instructing me that soon He'd send me a successor to the pastoral position at Shiloh, and I needed to make sure the transition went correctly and smoothly. At the time I was just looking for it to be over. However,

God said the church members needed to go through a proper transition of power because they had never seen nor been through the process. So we began a methodical approach as to who the next pastor would be. I helped them with forming a pastoral search committee, and I informed them of the proper requirements the incoming pastor needed to have. So when all was ready for me to do so, God allowed me to step down from the pastoral position at Shiloh Baptist Church and the transition of power in the church was smooth and easy.

Death of a Leader—Not The Death of A Ministry

When a leader in the ministry dies it is incumbent upon the church to find another leader as soon as possible. When Moses mentored Joshua, he held a public coronation for Joshua taking his role and the leader of the Israelites into the Promised Land. However, as Joshua became old he did no such thing. There was no coronation for a leader following him because none were selected.

Joshua 24:29-31 says, "Now it came to pass after these things that Joshua the son of Nun, the servant of the LORD, died, being one hundred and ten years old. And they buried him within the border of his inheritance at Timnath Serah, which is in the mountains of Ephraim, on the north side of Mount Gaash.

Israel served the LORD all the days of Joshua, and all the days of the elders who outlived Joshua, who had known all the works of the LORD which He had done for Israel."

As Joshua died before the other elders, it is logical to think he did not have time to prepare a proper successor. However, I have learned that mentors should always be on the lookout for sound protégés, and we should always be in the process of training our successors.

Once Joshua died, here begs the question: "Who will select our next leader? " Sure, the people had strong leaders. Caleb was still there along with the other elders who had led the conquest of the Israelites, but without the key leader selecting his replacement it caused a lot of infighting among the other leaders. While he was alive, Joshua had the tribes focused on fighting. However, as soon as he died, the Israelites began the slow descent into mediocrity, and they ultimately dropped the baton.

In Judges chapter 1, we see a truly sad sight. We begin to see Christian complacency and how it eats away at the moral fiber of the believer. If you want to stand strong in God and complete your mission, you should remember there are three areas we must be committed to:

- Committed to God and Christ — Foundational
- Committed to the Body of Christ — Relational
- Committed to the work of Christ — Operational

In Judges 1:27-36, we see how fast Christian complacency can destroy your destiny and your spiritual inheritance. If you do a slow review of the text, you will see the corruption of the enemy in the minds of the Israelite leaders. Represented are half of the tribes that entered into the Promised Land , but in their own way, each one showed the cracks of corruption in their spiritual dealings. Manasseh, Ephraim, and Naphtali did not drive out these heathen tribes as God said. Instead, they decided to put them under tribute and force them to pay. Ephraim, Zebulun, and Asher decided it was easier to live with the enemy rather than drive them out of the territory; thereby, Satan was granted a small foothold to remain within their territory.

The Job Is Not Over Until It's Over

Keep in mind when God instructed the Israelites as to their duties in conquering the Promised Land, His orders were clear and concise. However, the ease of a more comfortable lifestyle caused the tribes to turn from God, and ultimately, it brought about their destruction.

Judges 2:20-23 says, "Then the anger of the LORD was hot against Israel; and He said, 'Because this nation has transgressed My covenant which I commanded their fathers, and has not heeded My voice, I also will no longer drive out before them any of the nations which Joshua left when he died, so that through them I may test Israel, whether they will keep the ways of the LORD, to walk in them as their fathers kept them, or not.' Therefore the LORD left those nations, without driving them out immediately; nor did He deliver them into the hand of Joshua."

Children of God, it's a sad thing to have the authority of God in your hand but refuse to use it. You have the ability to accomplish so much more in your life but you refuse to because of laziness.

God was extremely angry with His children. I expect any parent would be too. Maybe you made a way for your children to succeed in life, but in return, they quit college; or maybe you cut back on your living to give your child that great gift and they dismissed all your hard work.

I remember once in my early years of growing up on our farm that Saturdays were days I dreaded. For many kids, Saturdays were days of watching their favorite cartoons or lounging around on their couches. However, for my brother and me it was a day of intense work either wrestling cows, bush hogging weeds, or fixing fences. And on the off chance we didn't have to do these jobs for our family, sometimes we were "lent out" to help others in the community wrestle their cows, bush hog their fields, or fix their fences.

Now please don't get me wrong. My brother and I enjoyed this time of our lives because we had fun doing the things we did, but I must admit those days were full of hard work.

I remember one crisp fall Saturday when we had worked from sunup to sundown. Whenever we had to work with our cows we generally started with them first, and that meant getting up with the chickens. Usually our dad would arouse us while it was still dark, and he would go and gather the cows by himself. As we matured, he started taking us with him and I loved going to the Old House as we called it.

The Old House is my grandfather's property that he leased for years, and God saw fit that his son, my father, was able to purchase the land for us . Now it stands as an inheritance for my children. Anyway, when my father began taking us with him he would always drive slowly onto the property, and he would begin to press on the horn in the truck.

As soon as the cows heard the sound of the horn, they would come running from all around our property because the honking horn meant they would be fed. As soon as the cows began coming to the pen where we would work them, many would keep walking with no inhibitions because they wanted some food. However, there were always some stragglers that held back and they wouldn't come to the pen too quickly.

When we had cows like this, it was always my brother's job and my job to wrangle these stragglers. What we would do was circle around the cows, get behind them, and slowly guide them into the pen. When we did this, sometimes the cows would try to run away from us because they knew going into the pen could mean a lot of different things for them. They could get shots, they could be sold, they could be worked, and since they did not know what was going to happen they would be pretty flighty.

Anyway, once we had all the cows, which usually numbered between sixty and eighty, we would get to work. Typically, it was non-stop for three or four hours as we gave shots to some, we circumcised others, we sold some, we tagged others, but all were worked in that four hours. From the smallest calf to the biggest bull, you had to stand your ground in the pen and make sure all of them were healthy. Now sometimes things didn't go as planned.

Every once in awhile you would run into a cow that was crazy, so you always had to be on your guard. When you work with animals that can weigh one thousand pounds you have to be careful.

Well, on this fateful day while working the morning away, I thought about going fishing once we were finished or riding my horse, but those thoughts came to a crashing halt pretty soon after we finished working our cows.

As we loaded the cows we were selling into the trailer, my dad said for us to go back to our house, get one of our tractors, and go bush hog our neighbor's land. Instantly I knew I was in trouble. The drive to our neighbors land was about five miles away but on a tractor, in the middle of the day when you have to dodge eighteen wheelers on an old two lane country road, it could take up to an hour. So I figured two hours there and back plus four to five hours of work would be most of my day.

As my brother and I drove to get the tractor, I thought about how much fun I could have following my own plans like horseback riding or fishing, but that wasn't in my father's plans. See, my father's plans did not consist of a life of ease but a life of responsibility and determination. I remember asking my dad that day when would we be finished, and he said, "The job's not over until it's over."

As we read about the Israelites, we see that they ultimately quit on God. Their leadership thought it would be better for them to suffer a life of ease rather than fulfill God's commands, and ultimately it cost them dearly.

What is it about God that when we disobey we immediately have dire consequences? If they had passed the test the first time there would have been no need for them to be tested by the enemies of God. God is saying, since you did not complete your task, I will leave them as a thorn in your side and their entire responsibility is to test you and make you suffer.

Do you know that once you break your word to God He is no longer bound by the promises He has made? Let's look at the text. We know God said, 'I will drive the inhabitants of the land out before you,' but since the Israelites chose a life of complacency and ease, God said, 'Well, since you won't do your part, I won't do my part.'

Now, please understand: God still loves you and He still sent His Son to die on the cross for you , but once you break your word with God, He is under no obligation to protect you from hurt, harm, and danger.

The Lost Generation

In 2012, I went on a life changing missionary trip to Dakar, Africa. Just flying into Dakar and seeing the nation where life began was soul stirring. When we landed in the airport and we passed customs, we were immediately shown to our two truck transportation and were on our way to Dahara where we set up to provide medical supplies to the indigenous population. All week we were whisked from location to location serving the people of Dahara, and by the end of the week I was worn to a frazzle.

As we were about to start preparing to come back to America, we decided to go to the local community shopping area. This is where the local farmers, merchants, and fishermen would come to sell their products, foods, and gifts. As we were entering this area, we were greeted by the local community and entreated to buy some of their products. As we traveled from area to area, I noticed a small group of about ten boys ranging from around four to ten years of age following our every move and continuously asking for alms.

Our guide noticed me watching these boys as they would go from person to person asking for some type of handout. During that short moment, she came over to me and said, "Those are the lost boys." When I asked her what that meant, she said, "They are the forgotten ones. They are boys who are given away to their local religious leaders within their first few years of birth and they are abandoned and forced to beg, borrow, and steal to survive."

When I learned of this situation my heart broke. Because of the parents' lack of fostering love and protection, their children grew up never knowing their true heritage. They never grew up knowing the strength of their fathers and mothers.

Well, this was how things turned out for the unknown generation of Joshua 2:10. The text says, " When all that generation had been gathered to their fathers, another generation arose after them who did not know the LORD nor the work which He had done for Israel."

Do you know how terrible it must be growing up not knowing who you are? Not knowing you are the wealth of a nation, but you are instead lost because those who were to protect you failed in their duty? And please do not believe this is just an "Africa thing." Here in the USA, we have our own set of "lost boys and lost girls." Our children are being forced into prostitution, selling drugs, and they are forced to rob and murder because the older generation of mentors failed the younger generation of protégés.

Is it so surprising that our world is in the state it is in? I tell you the truth, if our older generation of mentors decided to show us the way, instead of telling us the way, our world would be vastly different.

When I first began writing this book I always eyed writing this portion of it through eyes of anger. I always wanted to "shake the snot" out of the lost generation, but through my study I have found the lost generation of believers did not happen overnight. This generation was lost because the predecessor forgot the responsibility and determination it took to fight the good fight of faith.

So instead of looking at them with eyes of anger, I look at them with eyes of shame and pity but with hope as well. I believe every society has its version of "the lost boys." I believe every nation has those who they are ashamed of, but instead of pointing the finger at them and saying "pull your pants up and be a man," maybe we should walk up beside them, esteem them, and teach them what it means to be a man.

How can we teach our children how to love the Lord when the love of Christ isn't even in our own hearts? The failure of this generation does not rest at their feet. It rests at ours.

Do you remember earlier in this chapter when we discussed the acquiescence of sin? Do you remember how each tribe decided it wasn't worth the fight and chose to live with the sin instead of dealing with it? Inevitably, it destroyed an entire generation of believers.

This group of Israelites were so spiritually corrupt that the text says, "Then the children of Israel did evil in the sight of the LORD, and served the Baals; and they forsook the LORD God of their fathers, who had brought them out of the land of Egypt; and they followed other gods from among the gods of the people who were all around them, and they bowed down to them; and they provoked the LORD to anger."

Do you see why God had a "no holds barred" mentality when it comes to sin? You can't play with sin. You can't live with sin.

You must kill sin or it will kill you. These men and women decided that Jehovah wasn't enough of a God to them, so they decided to follow the god of the people who were left to be spiritual thorns to them.

In Exodus 20:5, God declared Himself jealous. If that wasn't enough of a warning, in His final discourse to the people of God before his death, Moses told them to pay attention to the God they served. Deuteronomy 4:23-26 says, "Take heed to yourselves, lest you forget the covenant of the LORD your God which He made with you, and make for yourselves a carved image in the form of anything which the LORD your God has forbidden you. For the LORD your God is a consuming fire, a jealous God. When you beget children and grandchildren and have grown old in the land, and act corruptly and make a carved image in the form of anything, and do evil in the sight of the LORD your God to provoke Him to anger, I call heaven and earth to witness against you this day, that you will soon utterly perish from the land which you cross over the Jordan to possess; you will not prolong your days in it, but will be utterly destroyed."

First, they should always take heed to their spiritual walk. He said, "Take heed for yourself." How much easier would our lives be if we took our spiritual temperatures every day?

Second, Moses told them the first step of sinning is forgetting you are in a covenant relationship with God. He said, "lest you forget the covenant of the LORD your God which He made with you." It is imperative that we keep our word to God the best way we can. The problem with many of us is we do not seek to renew our covenant with God.

When Christ gave us the two ordinances of the church, which are the Lord's Supper and Baptism, He made a special request at the end of the Lord's Supper. He said as recorded in 1 Corinthians 11:25, "In the same manner He also took the cup after supper, saying, 'This cup is the new covenant in My blood. This do, as often as you drink it, in remembrance of Me. For as often as you eat this bread and drink this cup, you proclaim the Lord's death till He comes.'"

Do you see that Christ spoke of the necessity of honoring the Lord's Supper often? True, He did not put any time frame on this except for us to do it often and for us to remember Him. What do you think would be the outcome of our lives if we always thought about Christ and we sought to remember our covenants with Him? Would we have generations of lost boys and girls being birthed into the world? No. I believe we would be that glorious church that He is coming back for that doesn't have spot or a wrinkle (Ephesians 5:27).

The third thing Moses sought to warn us about is making gods out of the things we see. He said, do not " make for yourselves a carved image in the form of anything which the LORD your God has forbidden you." Why would Moses stress this? It's because we as a people desire the things which we can see and touch. Since they had just left Egypt He knew the type of worship God hated and they were walking right back into an environment that derailed their faith in God.

Even in today's society we make gods out of our possessions. Our cars are our gods, our homes are our gods, and even our bodies become our gods. We must not put anything before the Lord. Why does Moses sternly warn them? Because God is a jealous God! No parent wants to be abused by their children and our heavenly Father is no different. He is a God who desires our love and our obedience, not our arrogance and unyielding hearts. Finally, Paul makes a point that every Christian needs to understand. To reap the blessing of God requires a "what have you done for me lately" mentality with

God. You can't get the future blessings of God on your past merits. It doesn't work that way as we will discover in our last chapter.

To be in the favor of God requires a daily walk and not last year's testimony. For us to keep strong in God we have to play straight with God. Notice when Moses spoke to the Children of Israel about moving away from God he gave them a span of three generations.

Moses knew three things had to take place for the total destruction of a generation. First, they would have to grow complacent; second, their complacency would lead to the experimenting with new things resulting in idol worship; and third, they would begin to sin openly by declaring these false gods as their true leaders and that would bring God's wrath on this "lost generation."

Study Guide

Chapter 5: The Dropped Baton

1. Have you ever dropped the baton? Have you ever dropped the thing that keeps you connected with God? Why or why not?

2. Who are you training to take your place in ministry? Who will be able to carry on in your position after God moves you?

3. What does this statement mean to you: "Only those who are expendable are promotable by God"? Explain what "expendable" means as well as what "promotable" means. How are the two tied together?

4. After Joshua succeeded Moses what are some of the causes that you see that could cause them to completely forget their need for another generation of leaders?

5. Define complacency and list five ways to keep from being complacent. Discuss them among your groups.

Chapter 6

PASSING THE MANTLE OF LEADERSHIP

Then he took the mantle of Elijah that had fallen from him, and struck the water, and said, "Where is the LORD God of Elijah?" And when he also had struck the water, it was divided this way and that; and Elisha crossed over.

—II Kings 2:14

"A leader is one who knows the way, goes the way, and shows the way."

—John C. Maxwell

In this chapter, I will spend some time talking about passing the mantle of leadership. This is always a difficult thing for any mentor or protégé because both have to be spiritually in line and open to receive from the other. To address this issue in the body of Christ, I would like to look at the relationship between Elijah and Elisha.

Elijah was a man of exceptional spiritual strength. However, he was also spiritually weak. In the presence of a king, he was steadfast and unmovable; but outside his comfort zone, he was easily shaken. Elijah was one of the most famous and dramatic prophets. However, he often chose to work alone and that led to times of isolation and loneliness.

We are introduced to the gruff prophet Elijah in I Kings 17:1. We encounter him already in ministry as we see him striding boldly into the palace of Ahab and informing him there wouldn't be any rain for three years. This prophecy was pronounced by God upon the wicked leadership of Ahab and Jezebel who served Baal and Asherah. It was a direct blow against Baal and Asherah worship as many considered them to be the gods of rain and bountiful blessings.

When Baal and Asherah worship became the practice of Ahab, God sent Elijah to Ahab to teach him who really was in charge. God said in Jeremiah 2:6-8, "Neither did they say, 'Where is the LORD, Who brought us up out of the land of Egypt, Who led us through the wilderness, Through a land of deserts and pits, Through a land of drought and the shadow of death, Through a land that no one crossed And where no one dwelt?' I brought you into a bountiful country, To eat its fruit and its goodness. But when you entered, you defiled My land and made My heritage an abomination. The priests did not say, 'Where is the LORD?' And those who handle the law did not know Me; The rulers also transgressed against Me; The prophets prophesied by Baal, And walked after things that do not profit."

We understand Ahab was a king who valued military might. However, this battle was not physical but spiritual. For all of his personal strength and the strength of his army, he was powerless to bring rain. While on the other hand, Elijah, who had no army or military might, possessed a strong spirit, and he was able to bring rain in the presence of all the people.

When it comes to respect, our God will not be disrespected by His children. When God responded to Ahab, He responded in word and deed.

When Elijah decreed this Word from God in the presence of Ahab, God instantly hid Elijah. He told him to go to the east and to stay at the brook Cherith where he would be hidden from Ahab. The brook of Cherith was hidden in the wilderness. It was a wild place for a wild man. It was a place that few people would go because of the difficulty of the area and the surrounding terrain.

While at the brook of Cherith we see the power of God manifested two fold. First, we see the miracle by the brook, and second, we see the miracle of the ravens.

It is a common belief that the brook was a seasonal brook. Sometimes it held water and sometimes it did not. During the summer months, this would have been the time that the brook would dry up. However, many believe Elijah was here by the brook for eighteen months. Do you see the spiritual implications here? Although Elijah had to flee for his life, God still spiritually sustained him during the first half of the drought in Israel by making sure a brook that normally would dry out would keep flowing and thus would sustain Elijah's life!

Are you in a drought? Do you know even in your lean times it is God who is supporting and sustaining you? Yes, you might not be where you want to be, but you have to know that God is still supplying your necessities by your spiritual brook of Cherith.

Second, we see God commanding the ravens to feed the prophet by the brook (I Kings 17:2). This was a very unusual miracle because ravens are unclean scavenger birds. In a nation where the people were charged to take care of the prophets, God assigned some unclean animals and a broken down widow to take care of the man of God.

In this setting alone, we see that God would rather use an unclean but obedient animal to perform His will than an unclean person who believes they are right with God. Now this is an unusual miracle but please do not think it strange. When God is working, as the Scriptures say, "all things are possible for them who believe" (Mark 9:23).

After the first eighteen months of his isolation, the brook began to dry up. Notice that by this time Elijah had come to rely and to depend on God's blessings by the brook. But as his season was drying up, God was silent. During times like this, our spirits should be cautious and careful with the things of God. For many people, when they see their blessings drying up their first instinct is to question God. But notice God did not say anything to Elijah until the brook was completely dry.

Remember, this is a walk of faith, and patience shows strength. We must maintain our faith during the droughts of our lives.

When God spoke to Elijah again He informed him He was sending him to a widow in Zarephath. Now, this is very ironic because of the location of Zarephath. When God instructed Elijah to flee from Ahab, He said for him to go eastward to the brook of Cherith. Now that the brook was dry, God was sending Elijah westward to Zarephath which was on the other side of Ahab's kingdom. Yes, to get to his destination he would have to walk through enemy territory.

As you are reading this book, I surmise some of you feel like you are walking through enemy territory. Are the friends whom you thought had your back turning on you? Are you being mistreated because the president elected isn't your boss's selection? Are you being persecuted because of your color? Or your style of dress?

Sometimes, God will have you walk through enemy territory to get to your destination. Just keep in mind, if God says your destination is on the other side, then be assured that you are going to make it!

For the second half of his three years in exile he lived with the widow of Zarephath. For the pious Jews, this would rank as one of those things that should never happen. According to Old Testament Law, the man of God was never to be alone in the presence of an unmarried woman. When Christ mentioned God sent Elijah to the widow of Zarephath in His first sermon, it incensed the people to the point where they tried to kill Christ.

Luke 4:26-30 says, "Then He said, 'Assuredly, I say to you, no prophet is accepted in his own country. But I tell you truly, many widows were in Israel in the days of Elijah, when the heaven was shut up three years and six months, and there was a great famine throughout all the land; but to none of them was Elijah sent except to Zarephath, in the region of Sidon, to a woman who was a widow. And many lepers were in Israel in the time of Elisha the prophet, and none of them was cleansed except Naaman the Syrian.' So all those in the syn-

Dr. Rayford E. Malone

agogue, when they heard these things, were filled with wrath, and rose up and thrust Him out of the city; and they led Him to the brow of the hill on which their city was built, that they might throw Him down over the cliff.

Then passing through the midst of them, He went His way." Understand how explosive of a situation God is sending Elijah into. Elijah knew according to the Law, he should not be in the house with the widow. However, what God decrees, as a child of God, we should follow. Because of Elijah's obedience, God blessed him, the widow, and her house during his stay in Zarephath.

At the end of the eighteen months, God speaks to Elijah and sends him back into Ahab's kingdom. Upon speaking to the king, Elijah calls for the king, the people, and the prophets of Baal and Asherah to meet him on Mount Carmel. When the people arrive Elijah places a choice before the people of God: If you want to choose God then choose Him; If you want to choose Baal and Asherah choose them; But stop being lukewarm.

I find it incredibly sad that the people did not respond to Elijah's charge. Although they knew Jehovah was God they had allowed themselves to slip into a moral stupor by serving Baal and Asherah. I surmise if the people responded to God favorably there would be no need for the sacrifice. However, their indecision moved Elijah to take the next step which allowed God to demonstrate His power.

Sometimes, people need to see the awesomeness of God instead of just hearing about it.

Elijah then issues a challenge. Each side would prepare a sacrifice and whoever's sacrifice was accepted by fire falling from Heaven that God would be the people's God. Notice in I Kings 18:25 that Elijah allows the false prophets to go first while he sits quietly by. Elijah let the prophets of Baal choose the ox they wanted to use. He then let them get their altar together. He let them sacrifice the animal. They spread the animal out on the altar, and they start calling on their gods. Nothing happens. This group of prophets would beat themselves with a cat o' nine tails that would have lit tle metal pieces in it. So as they're beating themselves, the blood is streaming down their backs, because they believed the blood would cause a god to act in their existence right then at that time.

Around noontime (1Kings 18:27), Elijah is seen enjoying the performance of the false prophets. The text says he began to mock them in the presence of the people because their god had not shown up.

The Bible says about evening time, toward the end of the time for the sacrifice, Elijah took twelve stones and rebuilt the torn down altar. He dug a trench around the altar, put the animal on top of the altar, and he commanded the people, "Now get four buckets of water." And he commanded them to drench the altar and the sacrifice in water twelve times. Now I find it interesting that Elijah would only ask the people to do this one task in preparing the sacrifice.

The number twelve stood for the unity of the Israelites' twelve tribes. They used twelve stones for the foundation and twelve buckets of water to drench the sacrifice symbolically demonstrating the coming of the Holy Spirit.

Then Elijah went over to the side, got on his hands and knees, and started interceding for the people that they would realize that Jehovah is God, and, like many of us, they needed to see a demonstration of His power. The Bible says that as soon as he finished praying, fire from Heaven came down. It burned up everything. It burned up the animal, it burned up the stones, and it burned up all the water.

First Kings 18:39 says, "Now when all the people saw it, they fell on their faces; and they said, 'The Lord, He is God! The Lord, He is God!'" Then Elijah has the people perform an act of faith that shows a symbolic breaking away from Baal worship. He has them kill all the prophets of Baal and Asherah.

With this done, Elijah went up to the mountain to pray and God sent a torrent upon the country. Here we see the strength of Elijah. He called fire down from Heaven. But in the next few verses we see the weakness of Elijah.

First Kings 19:1-4 says, "And Ahab told Jezebel all that Elijah had done, also how he had executed all the prophets with the sword. Then Jezebel sent a messenger to Elijah, saying, 'So let the gods do to me, and more also, if I do not make your life as the life of one of them by tomorrow about this time.' And when he saw that, he arose and ran for his life, and went to Beersheba, which belongs to Judah, and left his servant there. But he himself went a day's journey into the wilderness, and came and sat down under a broom tree. And he prayed that he might die, and said, 'It is enough! Now, LORD, take my life, for I am no better than my fathers!'"

This text is full of spiritual depth. But for now, I want to concentrate on the actions of Elijah. Upon hearing her threat, his first instinct was to flee. Now when we look at Elijah, the first question that comes to mind is, Why? Why would he need to flee from Jezebel? His God had just protected him for three years when the land was in drought. He protected him during the spiritual warfare he endured on Mt. Carmel, and surely He would have protected him from Jezebel.

Verse 3 says, "And he was afraid and arose and ran for his life." He did not stop to think that the same God who could allow fire to come from Heaven to eat up an altar and the sacrifice he had just made the very day before could deliver him from Jezebel. That is how bad Jezebel was in his mind. That's how much of a stumbling block to Elijah, Jezebel was. He could, the very day before, do something that had never been done before when he prayed and called on the name of God, and then as soon as he hears her voice, everything inside of him is gone.

Oftentimes in life, we pray to God about things and God moves miraculously. Then the very next day, a trial comes along, and we get shaken in our faith to the point where we don't even know how to act. We get to the place where we start talking bad to folk, and we know we are supposed to be Christians, saved by grace through faith. You know God is on your side, but as soon as the enemy speaks in your life the first thing you do is take off running.

Now, Jezebel couldn't put a hand on Elijah because Elijah was anointed. He was saved by God. Didn't we see evidence of God's divine protection when he was at the Brook of Cherith? The only thing she could do was speak a word to let him know she was trying to kill him. It messed him up. I have a word for everybody reading this: the enemy wants to kill every one of you. So now, when you hear the voice of the enemy speaking in your life, you already know what he is trying to do. It's his assignment.

But the Bible tells us, "No weapon that is formed against you will prosper." So many times in life we get afraid just because the enemy makes the weapon. If the enemy can't prosper, why sweat over his making the weapon? Sometimes, we get so afraid when we see the enemy sharpening a blade or an ax or something, but God says it's not going to prosper. In spite of that, we get to the place where we start to run from a Jezebel in our lives.

Elijah didn't give God a chance to protect him because he immediately ran for his life. And, once he made it to Beersheba, he left his servant there. It is a dangerous thing when a man of God decides to walk this pathway alone. However, there are times when we have to end relationships with certain servants because they can't travel the same pathway. Maybe they are too inexperienced, or too full of ego, or maybe they just aren't the right fit; but you will know soon if they can make the journey you are called to travel.

Please notice I did not call this man who walked with Elijah a protégé. I called him a servant. In the relationship between Moses and Joshua, we see that Joshua started off as a servant, he then became a protégé, and he eventually ended up an equal who led the Children of Israel into their Promised Land. However, this man began as a servant and he ended as a servant. Why? Apparently, he did not have what it takes to walk with Elijah.

Some theologians believe this young servant was the resurrected son of the widow of Zarephath. Others believe it is a young Jonah.

Here is a word for pastors and ministry leaders: Every person who comes and walks with you isn't your protégé. Many are there to learn for a season, but they never grow past their servant role. As a pastor, I have seen many men and women of God come to the church or department and the same gifts and talents they brought to the table are the same gifts and talents they take with them when they leave. They never strive to grow or expand their horizons. As a pastor, I seek to learn what the ministers of the House desire to do, and I often seek ways that I can help them reach their individual goals. I have learned, however, that many people are content to stay right where they are. They are content in their relationship, and they never seek to advance or expand on their gift.

Here is one thing God has taught me about the heart of a true servant versus one who is content. As a pastor and prison chaplain, I am able to bring in ministers to preach for me in either setting. However, when I meet a preacher who I am potentially interested in, I always ask him to preach in the prison first. The reason I do this is because the prison is a place for true ministry, and it's a place where you won't receive human praise, but you will receive spiritual praise.

Usually, when I make this offer, I am turned down. Maybe one out of ten will accept, and that lets me know the heart of the person that I am dealing with. Those who turn down the prison invite never get the opportunity to preach in the church setting because, as a servant of God, we should be willing to go and share our gifts and talents wherever God opens the door.

In my time as a pastor and chaplain, I am shocked by the number of preachers who tell me, "God did not call me to prison ministry," and they are right. God called them to ministry, period! Christ said when we visit those in prison it's as if we are visiting Him. Matthew 25:34-40 says, " Then the King will say to those on His right hand, 'Come, you blessed of My Father, inherit the kingdom prepared for you from the foundation of the world: for I was hungry and you gave Me food; I was thirsty and you gave Me drink; I was a stranger and you took Me in; I was naked and you clothed Me; I was sick and you visited Me; I was in prison and you came to Me.' Then the righteous will answer Him, saying, 'Lord, when did we see You hungry and feed You, or thirsty and give You drink? When did we see You a stranger and take You in, or naked and clothe You? Or when did we see You sick, or in prison, and come to You?' And the King will answer and say to them, 'Assuredly, I say to you, inasmuch as you did it to one of the least of these My brethren, you did it to Me.'"

This text is showing us that possessing a servant's heart is mandatory to fulfilling the work of the ministry. There's no pay in visiting the prison. There's no honorarium for clothing strangers. There's no special "get out of jail free card" that comes with feeding the poor. However, Scriptures tell us God is watching all that we do and He will bless us for it. Matthew 5:16 says, "Let your light so shine before men, that they may see your good works and glorify your Father in heaven."

And to those who don't have a servant's attitude, He says in Matthew 25:41-46: "Then He will also say to those on the left hand, 'Depart from Me, you cursed, into the everlasting fire prepared for the devil and his angels: for I was hungry and you gave Me no food; I was thirsty and you gave Me no drink; I was a stranger and you did not take Me in, naked and you did not clothe Me, sick and in prison and you did not visit Me.' Then they also will answer Him, saying, 'Lord, when did we see You hungry or thirsty or a stranger or naked or sick or in prison, and did not minister to You?' Then He will answer them, saying,

'Assuredly, I say to you, inasmuch as you did not do it to one of the least of these, you did not do it to Me.' And these will go away into everlasting punishment, but the righteous into eternal life."

As I said earlier, there will be plenty who will attempt to serve Christ, but they won't go all the way with you. There are plenty of ministers whom God will send to you who don't have the heart of a protégé. When you see that you have a servant who isn't willing to pay the price to be a protégé, it's best to leave them in Beersheba.

Then the text informs us of Elijah: "But he himself went a day's journey into the wilderness, and came and sat down under a broom tree." Some journeys are treacherous especially when we decide to walk alone. I believe when we run from our issues and doubt, no matter how far or how fast we run, we will always wind up alone in the wilderness. We know the wilderness can be dangerous for a stressed mentor.

Sure you know the Word, sure you have God on your side, but no preacher should be in the wilderness too long. God has called us to live our lives in the light. However, when we are in the wilderness sometimes we begin to do things that are sinful. This is why you must be careful in your wilderness. Often times we begin to backslide because we grow accustomed to the darkness in our wilderness instead of fighting against it.

Finally, Elijah took a moment, and he did the one thing he should have done before he began running from his issues. He prays. While he sits under a juniper tree he bows his head in prayer. However, notice his prayer was one not seeking God for protection but one calling out the shame he felt in his own life for missing the mark of God. First Kings 19:4 says, "And he prayed that he might die, and said, 'It is enough! Now, LORD, take my life, for I am no better than my fathers!'"

Do you see the heart-brokenness in his prayer? Now I, for one second, don't believe Elijah wanted to die. If death was his goal, I am sure he would have run to Jezebel and not from Jezebel. If death was his desire, all he had to do once he heard her threat was to sit down and wait for his executioner, but he did not do any of these things. So we see that plea for seeking death is not an option, but despair and hopelessness are. Here this gruff prophet was shamed, broken, and depressed, so he asks God to take his life. And notice, God doesn't even entertain the question because it is silliness to God. God has an assignment for each of us to do and His will supersedes ours.

Talk about riding a wave of emotion! One second you're riding the most powerful crest of the wave and the next you're experiencing the depth of the trough only to be battered against the rocks of self pity. Can you imagine in one moment shouting, "The Lord, He is God," and in the next you are running for your life!

Oftentimes, when we reach that spiritual low, God begins to move in our lives because it's not over. We choose when we lie down and say, "I'm through." But oftentimes, we're not through according to God. We can hit that place where we just say, "I'm done. I have tried and I have tried and I have tried. I tried to keep my heart right. I tried to keep this ministry running. I tried to tell you I love you. I tried…"

Repeat these words out loud: "I tried to tell you don't be mad. I tried to tell you I'm working on this thing. I tried to tell you I have problems. I'm trying and I'm trying and I'm trying. Now I'm finished." As he lay there and slept, I found it odd that it was an angel God sent, but not God Himself. The angel stirs him, and the angel says, "Arise, eat." Elijah gets up.

Now the presence of the angel serves two things. One, it shows us that God values us as children of God, and two, God needed Elijah to complete his tasks.

Notice this is the second time Elijah ran from Ahab, and both times when he ran, he ran to deserted places. When God shut up Heaven for three years, he ran to the wilderness, and he was fed by the ravens. After a time, God moved him to Zarephath, and now, this third time, he is being visited by an angel. And all the while God was in control.

God sent the ravens, God sent the widow, and God sent the angel. Through each step in the journey, God was guiding him and bringing him closer to the revelation of who He is in his life.

Now understand what he has just blessed him with. Even though this is a spiritual matter, God still provides for him in the physical sense. He still gives him food, and He still gives him water. As soon as he eats and drinks, he lies back down again. Then the angel comes right back, wakes him up again, and says, "Arise, eat, because the journey is too great for you." The angel is God's representative. Sometimes, God can't speak to us because of our weak spiritual condition, so He will send people or angels to speak His Words into our lives.

Here's a funny story I heard in seminary. There was once a man whose favorite catchphrase was " I'm waiting on God." Whenever someone asked him a question about the future, he would say, "I'm waiting on God." If they asked him who would win the latest football game, he'd say, "I'm waiting on God." Well, one day a powerful storm came and flood waters began circling his house so he climbed on the roof and he prayed and he said, "God, if you're God, save me." So then a man came by in a boat. He says, "Hey, come on, jump in the boat with me." The guy says, "No, I'm waiting on God." So the guy in the boat went on about his business, and the water kept rising. Soon another man in a boat came by, and he says, "Hey, jump in the boat because the water is rising." He says, "No, I'm waiting on God." The second boatman sailed off shaking his head. About thirty minutes later, the water was up to the top of the house and a helicopter flies over. The guy in the helicopter is like, "Hey, come up! The water is about to go over the house." The guy says, "No, I'm waiting on God." So the helicopter flies away.

The guy eventually drowns and when he's standing at the pearly gates he demands to know where God was! He says, "God, I was waiting on You to save me. Why didn't You come and save me?" God says, "Hey, I sent by two people in the boat and the helicopter."

God sends angels to us throughout our lives, but oftentimes we don't recognize them. The Bible tells us, "Watch how you treat people because you could be entertaining angels unaware." You don't know who they are.

In this Scripture, it tells us this was definitely an angel that had to deliver a word, but often in life our angels are people we don't even know who come in and speak a word to us at our lowest point just to give us some encouragement and hope. And here in this text, he tells him, "Arise, eat, because this journey is too great for you."

I would have asked him, "What is the journey? What is the problem? What is so great? Is it greater than God?" The only thing that was greater than Elijah at this time was his accessibility to allow fear to dominate who he was. It wasn't that his fear was more powerful than he was, because you saw how the Word of God operated in his life. God used him as a conduit, but he allowed his fear of Jezebel to shake him to the point where he lost all sense of who he was as God's servant and his mission in the earth.

So my question is: What is it you're doing that you're trying to do in your own power, in your own strength that is too great for you? Was this a moment of regression for Elijah?

The angel said, "It's so great for you." The angel has to give him a spiritual word and physical food. The Bible says once he received that word, he ran for forty days and forty nights, but he had to accept that his journey, what he was doing, was too much for him. He couldn't do it by himself. He had to know the only way he was going to make it through was through God, because the same God who delivered him the day before was the same God who would deliver him tomorrow.

We get messed up because it's the same God who deals with our issues of today. We say, "Okay, I remember what He used to do and I know His promises for the future," but we don't worry about what he is doing right now. It's the same God who is sustaining you right now. The same One who gets you up in the morning. The same One who has you sitting here right now. He is the same God who sustains you. If He did it yesterday and He can do it tomorrow, He can do it today.

We often think the trial we're in is so big and so great we can't get out of it. God says, "What's the problem? If I protected you yesterday, I can do it today." The only thing that is different is us. We are not in yesterday's trial. We are in today's trial and, with each new trial, comes a completely new set of circumstances. This is why a person can have faith when he or she loses a parent but crumble when he or she loses a job. Or they might stand strong in faith during a child's sickness, but when a person criticizes them, they lose their religion and distance themselves from God.

A lot of times people start thinking something is wrong, but they have to hear you say, "Wait, it's not that anything is wrong; it's just that I'm trying to hear from God. I can't hear from God with you in my ear always trying to tell me what to do, how to act, or where to go. I need to hear from God. So I love you, baby, but right now I have to close the door." You need to understand you're going to have to close the door on some folks in your life. It's not being mean. It's not being rude.

Sometimes you have to go in your closet. Sometimes, you have to say, "Baby, look. I love you, but I'm going through some things with God, so I have to get me right. In getting me right. I have to get in my closet. I have to get away from you. I know you love me, and I know you have the best interest for me in your mind, but what I need you to do for me is you need to start praying that I hear from God, not from you. If I keep hearing from you, I might mess up what God is trying to tell me." We have to get to this place where God speaks.

Now notice when the angel comes, he sees him, and he says, "This trial is too hard for you. Your journey is too long. I have to give you some spiritual food, and I have to give you some physical food." He is feeding the duality of this man. The first thing he did after he ate was he got up and he took off running for forty days and forty nights to Mount Horeb.

I submit to you, Elijah had this destination in mind the entire time he began running from Jezebel. If you do a study on Mount Horeb you will see that the Israelites seldom visited Mount Horeb. The last time it was used in any spiritual capacity was through the ministry of Moses, and Mount Horeb was holy ground. In the New Testament, we see a commonality between Moses and Elijah as they are seen with Christ on the Mount of Transfiguration. Moses represented the law, while Elijah represented the prophetic order. Also, the cave that Elijah passed the night in was the same cave that Moses stood by when he saw the Glory of God passing by.

This place had spiritual significance! I believe he knew this was the one place he could go and speak to God face-to-face. He knew he had to get to the one place where God spoke to him the most, and that was at Mount Horeb. The text teaches us when Elijah arrived God began to speak to him in this sacred place.

I believe God could have spoken to Elijah in the same place the angel spoke to him, but I believe he wasn't spiritually ready to receive from God.

When he got there, the first thing he heard was God talking to him. God did not go through a long thesis. He didn't try to address every situation in his life. He just asked him the only question that truly mattered. He said, "What are you doing here, Elijah?" What is it that has you running so much and so far and so fast that you are here now in front of Me? What is it?"

Now God could have spoken to the man way back over there in front of the juniper tree, but Elijah wasn't ready to hear from God. That's why God didn't speak to him. Do you have a sacred place? A place that is designated to meet God that's special to your soul? Maybe it's your closet or your church; but either way, Elijah held onto his hurt, grief, and pain until he was in front of God. For him to "let it all out," he needed to be at this special place.

A lot of times we think we're ready to hear what God has to say, but that isn't the case. Sometimes when God begins to speak to us, we start thinking it's the enemy talking to us and we try to rebuke God.

We pray, "God, please help me with this situation." God says, "Well, do this: Cut off some of your friends in your life." We say, "Well, I know that's the enemy because those are true friends of mine." God is really the one who is speaking. So God says, "Well, you're not ready to hear from Me, so I'm not even going to talk to you. I'm going to go ahead and send somebody else into your path to get your mind right."

Now, let's look at the question God asks Elijah. God says, "What are you doing here, Elijah?" God is all powerful and all knowing so we know God already knew the answer to the question. This question of God is more like a rebuke from God in the sense that Elijah was not in his proper place. Like any parent, it informs the child of two things. First, it lets the child know the parents are aware that they are somewhere spiritually, mentally, or physically that they are not supposed to be; and second, it lets the child have room to express himself openly to the parents; and third, it encourages the child to remember and return to his main duty and responsibilities. God was striving to get Elijah to return to his pathway of ministry.

Here's a motto I try to live by: If God is silent keep doing the last thing He said.

This statement by God to Elijah gives me the impression that God is expecting Elijah to be doing something totally different with his time. God was not expecting Elijah to be on Mount Horeb. God wasn't expecting Elijah to need angelic assistance. God wasn't expecting Elijah to run from Jezebel. God was expecting him to complete his mission which was to be a light for Israel during the darkest times of their history.

When Elijah addresses God he speaks from his fear. Notice that Elijah had just ran for forty days and forty nights. Also, he had just spent some time in the presence of one of God's angels, and even though he had been fed spiritually and physically by God, he was still trapped in the same spiritual dungeon.

Forty days is a long time to be in spiritual bondage.

In verse 10, we read, "I have been very zealous for the Lord, the God of hosts; for the sons of Israel have forsaken your covenant, torn down your altars and killed your prophets with the sword. And I alone am left; and they seek my life, to take it away." Notice that Elijah is proclaiming his innocence before God and how he alone has carried the banner for God while all the other prophets were killed.

When you look back over you life, do you see where God delivered you? Or do you see when you felt He had failed you? So many times in our lives we forget God's saving grace.

Instead of saying, "God, You delivered me. I know You kept me safe from every hurt, harm, and danger," we think about the bad times and we begin complaining to God about the pathway He has called us to follow. If you are on an extended journey, please stop looking at the bad times. Look at the good times God has delivered us from. Look at the good times, because I guarantee you there are more good times than there are bad times.

God tells him, "Go out on the side of the mountain. Then He said, 'Go out, and stand on the mountain before the LORD.' And behold, the LORD passed by, and a great and strong wind tore into the mountains and broke the rocks in pieces before the LORD, but the LORD was not in the wind; and after the wind an earthquake, but the LORD was not in the earthquake; and after the earthquake a fire, but the LORD was not in the fire; and after the fire a still small voice."

Please understand this text. God sending Elijah outside was to teach him, just as He did Moses, that there is a difference between the presence of God and the power of God. When Elijah stood on the side of the mountain, the first thing that passed by was God Himself. Sometimes we must learn that the presence of God can be around us and among us but we never know it. God's presence must be felt in our lives before we ever feel His power. Once the presence of God passed by God then begins to show Elijah His power. To see the power of God had to be a truly great and mighty thing. Elijah was privy to the powerful winds making the rocks crumble as He destroyed the mountains. He had to feel the strong earthquake that shook his feet. Last, he had to see the fire of God. But in all of these powerful examples God wasn't in them.

He is showing these great and terrible things in our lives.

You have this violent wind, you have this earthquake, and you have this fire—things in our lives that could be disastrous for us, things that could beat up and break everything we have going on. Then here comes a gentle blowing breeze. As soon as the breeze starts blowing, Elijah knew God was in the gentle breeze and he walked back outside.

The Passing of the Mantle

Saints, notice what Elijah does before he walked outside. He covered his face with his mantle. The text says, "So it was, when Elijah heard it, that he wrapped his face in his mantle and went out and stood in the entrance of the cave. Suddenly a voice came to him, and said, 'What are you doing here, Elijah?'"

Now, let's talk about Elijah's mantle because it is very important to us to focus on it for the remainder of the book. In the Old Testament, a person would wear a mantle for three main reasons:

- It's a sign of authority
- It was a sign of protection
- It could be used as a covering

When you read about the authority given to mighty men each had their symbol of Godly authority. Moses had a staff. Elijah had a mantle. Moses' staff parted the Red Sea, Elijah's staff parted the Jordan River.

Then God asked Elijah a second time, "What are you doing here, Elijah?" and his response was just as sad as the first time. "He said, 'I have been very zealous for the LORD God of hosts; because the children of Israel have forsaken Your covenant, torn down Your altars, and killed Your prophets with the sword. I alone am left; and they seek to take my life.'"

Our God does not deal in self-pity. Nor does He deal in self-denial. God had called Elijah to do a job but he was failing. But instead of removing Elijah from ministry, God gave him a protégé. God gave Elijah a new role as a teacher of Elisha. Notice, God never spoke to Elijah about his fear or his shame. God just called him right back to his duty with a more painful and severe rebuke for his hardheartedness.

Then the LORD said to him: "Go, return on your way to the wilderness of Damascus; and when you arrive, anoint Hazael as king over Syria. Also you shall anoint Jehu the son of Nimshi as king over Israel. And Elisha the son of Shaphat of Abel Meholah you shall anoint as prophet in your place. It shall be that whoever escapes the sword of Hazael, Jehu will kill; and whoever escapes the sword of Jehu, Elisha will kill. Yet I have reserved seven thousand in Israel, all whose knees have not bowed to Baal, and every mouth that has not kissed him."

When God sent Elijah away He told him to retrace his steps. Do you know if you ever run from the presence of God He will always have you retrace your steps. The farther you run the greater distance you have to travel to get right with God.

When many of us fall off the wagon in God we have to go through a recovery process. We have to make up for that lost time. One of the saddest things I have seen in ministry is men and women of God retracing their steps as they find their way back to God after running from Him.

Some of them ran for a year. Others ran for five or ten years. Once I met a man who said he ran from God for twenty years and his greatest regret was the lost time he spent hiding from God's presence. How many lives could he have touched? How many destinies could he have inspired? No one knows. Now, I praise God that he found his way back to the Lord but, sometimes, the "what ifs" in ministry really weigh you down.

God is letting Elijah know that his time is drawing to an end. It does not matter if it was "just his time to go" or if it was his refusal to see God's work in his life dealing with Jezebel was the breaking point. But in either case, God was preparing to remove him from this world and send him to the next. But he had to establish a mentor/ protégé relationship with someone to supersede him.

Now, the spiritual revelation of the 7,000 men has nothing to do with an exact number; it has to do with Elijah knowing that God had other men and women who were hidden from the evil of Ahab and Jezebel that God could use at any time. God has more servants, preachers, bishops, and overseers than we know. It is not for us to determine our value or worth by trying to assess our gifts which will lead us to being self righteous.

Now, please don't be worried about the wrong thing! God's work will be in operation a long time after we have gone home to Glory. We, as leaders and ministers of righteousness, are simply links in a chain. When you start to focus on yourself you show cracks in your link. Now, will the chain ever break? Absolutely not. As we learned, God would not allow the fire to go out in the time with Eli and Samuel, and He will not allow the chain to be broken with you or me.

So if you're having your pity party, thinking about all the hard work you are doing in the gospel ministry, I have two words for you: WAKE UP! The work of God will continue but the workers of God will retire to glory!

God is saying to Elijah, 'What I'm going to do is, when that 7,000 get where they need to be, those two kings are going to start going through the land and cutting off Baal left and right. If they get away from one king, I have the second king in line. If they get away from the second king, I have a prophet in line. So don't you worry about this, because I've got this covered.'

Notice God told Elijah who his successor would be although the two had never met. As soon as Elijah starts retracing his steps he meets his protégé.

The Long Walk of Ministry

As we begin to close this book, I would like to share with you that the long walk of ministry is a time of testing. This time is certainly true for the mentor as well as the protégé. As they are walking together they both will have tests and trials that they must overcome individually and together.

To express this point, I would like to talk to you about Elijah's last day on this side of Heaven. When you read II Kings chapter two, it opens with the grim report that God was going to take Elijah into Heaven in a whirlwind. This is fitting for Elijah because he began his ministry as a whirlwind, and it concluded in a whirlwind.

As we read about the towns Elijah and Elisha traveled through, each one has spiritual significance to the mentor/ protégé bond. Second Kings 2:2 says, "Then Elijah said to Elisha, 'Stay here, please, for the Lord has sent me on to Bethel.' But Elisha said, 'As the Lord lives, and as your soul lives, I will not leave you!' So they went down to Bethel."

The starting point of their journey is Gilgal. In Hebrew etymology, Gilgal means the place of the roll. In a figurative sense, it means to roll oneself onto the Lord (Psalm 22:8). When the Israelites entered the Promised Land, the men were circumcised in Gilgal. In this sense, their reproach for not obeying the Lord when He brought them to the Promised Land the first time was rolled away (Joshua 5:9).

When we review this text it seems everyone knows what's going on but no one wants to say it. Some scholars believe Elijah was trying to spare Elisha the heartbreak of seeing his mentor taken into Heaven. However, I believe this was a divine test from God. On this day, God took Elijah through three major towns, and it was only when they entered one city did God reveal it to Elijah to proceed to the next. With each city, Elisha was given the opportunity to stay. When you look at the mentor/protégé relationship, the protégé must remain with the mentor for the complete season for him to be able to walk in his anointing.

Notice, when Elisha was given the opportunity to leave Elijah he steadfastly refused. Maybe because he knew the only way he could get the anointing that he desired in his life was to see the relationship to its completion.

In verse three, we see something very interesting in the text. It seems that everyone knew Elijah was going to be taken into Heaven that day but only Elisha was willing to walk with Elijah to the completion of the journey.

This is how we know Elisha was a true protégé. He did not run or decide to stay back. He simply continued on his journey following his mentor.

Upon arriving at Bethel, we are shown something new in this story. Bethel means the House of God. Along the walk of the mentor/protégé relationship, it is incumbent upon the mentor to show the protégé how to respect and operate in the House of God.

The sons of the prophets in Bethel knew Elijah was going to be taken away that very day. In II Kings 3:3, it says, "Now the sons of the prophets who were at Bethel came out to Elisha, and said to him, 'Do you know that the LORD will take away your master from over you today?'" Many scholars believe that Elijah was going from city to city to view the schools of the prophets, but this does not ring true to the text. The text shows us the prophets came out to Elijah and Elisha and all mentioned that Elijah would be taken that day, but none of the prophets were willing to complete the journey with Elijah and Elisha.

Sure they wanted Elisha to know that God was going to take Elijah, but they were not willing to pay the cost to travel with the man of God. From Bethel they traveled to Jericho, and we see the same scene played out again. In II Kings 2:4-5 , it says, "Then Elijah said to him, 'Elisha, stay here, please, for the LORD has sent me on to Jericho.' But he said, 'As the LORD lives, and as your soul lives, I will not leave you!' So they came to Jericho. Now the sons of the prophets who were at Jericho came to Elisha and said to him, 'Do you know that the LORD will take away your master from over you today?' So he answered, 'Yes, I know; keep silent!'"

If you have read your history of the Bible, you would know that Jericho is a cursed place. Spiritually speaking, this is one area in which every mentor needs to instruct his protégé, and that is spiritual warfare. In our day and time, spiritual warfare is sorely needed because so many of us refuse to engage in it.

Finally, God stops sending him to cities and he sends him to the Jordan. In II Kings 2:6-7, the text says, "Then Elijah said to him, 'Stay here, please, for the LORD has sent me on to the Jordan.' But he said, 'As the LORD lives, and as your soul lives, I will not leave you!'" So the two of them went on. And fifty men of the sons of the prophets went and stood facing them at a distance, while the two of them stood by the Jordan. For many of us, the Jordan River represents death. In the mentor/protégé role, the mentor must teach the protégé how to die to the flesh and not thrive in the flesh. As we grow more mature we must learn how to kill the flesh before it kills our spirits.

The Crossover

Now, here is another small spiritual nugget. Only Elijah and Elisha were willing to walk close to death. The other prophets would not even come close. This shows me a true mentor and protégé will travel wherever they must to reach their destination and goals. The other prophets were afraid to come near the Jordan.

The fact that at each destination Elijah tried to discourage Elisha from seeing him being taken by God speaks to the love this mentor had for his protégé. But on the other hand, it also shows Elisha's determination to seeing things all the way through with his mentor.

In preparing to cross the Jordan, Elijah rolls up his mantle, strikes the water, and they walk across on dry ground in the same way Moses stretched his staff over the Red Sea and the Israelites walked across on dry ground. The text says in II Kings 2:8, "Now Elijah took his mantle, rolled it up, and struck the water; and it was divided this way and that, so that the two of them crossed over on dry ground."

Notice during this entire dialogue, the only time Elijah asks Elisha what he wants is after they have made it through the trials in relationship. They have crossed death, and now they stand precariously awaiting Elijah's chariot.

Eye on the Prize

Saints, a true protégé will pay a price that other ministers, leaders, or prophets are willing to pay. The price that you must pay is determined by God but the willingness to pay that price is dependent upon the protégé.

When I was an armor bearer I used to take joy in being with my pastor when the other ministers were tired and would express a desire to go home. It was during those intimate times that I learned the most about ministry. When the hustle and bustle of church business or worship services were done I would ask my questions.

I knew well enough that when we were in the presence of others it was never a good time to ask my questions. The reason for this is I knew the "church answers" would be given to the babes who we shepherded on a week to week basis. But in the back office is where I would get the hard core truth.

Also, the text shows us that Elisha never asked for anything until Elijah offered. Notice their verbal exchange as soon as they crossed over: "And so it was, when they had crossed over, that Elijah said to Elisha, 'Ask! What may I do for you, before I am taken away from you?' Elisha said, 'Please let a double portion of your spirit be upon me.'"

On one hand, I know Elijah was shocked at Elisha's desire. His statement that "you have asked a hard thing" gives credence to the unexpectedness of the request. However, I believe any true father in the ministry desires for his sons to follow in his footsteps. Some argue over whether this double portion of spirit was from Elijah or if the double portion referred to was as if Elisha was Elijah's first born spiritual son. As we know, according to Old Testament law, the eldest son always received a double portion of the father's goods.

Notice, he did not ask for riches, fame, or fortune. He simply asked for more anointing to continue the work of the prophets. From our view, it looks as if the suggestion by Elisha shocks Elijah. So he said, "You have asked a hard thing. Nevertheless, if you see me when I am taken from you, it shall be so for you; but if not, it shall not be so." Then it happened, as they continued on and talked, that suddenly a chariot of fire appeared with horses of fire and separated the two of them; and Elijah went up by a whirlwind into Heaven.

What do you think it would look like to see your leader caught up in the presence of God? I know, as a young minister, when I would see my pastor being touched by God in the church or even when we were out at lunch it was a beautiful sight. It showed me that I needed to move closer to God.

I believe if more ministers would support their pastors they would see their leader caught up and it would be a blessing for the entire church.

Now Elijah knew that a double portion of his spirit was not his to give. That can only come from God. So in confirming his wishes, Elijah still gives God room to have his way even on this side of the Jordan. If Elisha saw him being caught up in the spirit then the double portion would be his. If not, then he would not receive the double portion.

As they talked and walked, the chariot divided them. The mentor/protégé relationship can only last so long. Sooner or later the mentor will precede the protégé on to glory and the protégé must take his place as a mentor. The Scripture tells us that Elisha not only saw Elijah taken into Heaven, but he also caught his falling mantle.

Second Kings 2:11-14 says, "And Elisha saw it, and he cried out, 'My father, my father, the chariot of Israel and its horsemen!' So he saw him no more. And he took hold of his own clothes and tore them into two pieces. He also took up the mantle of Elijah that had fallen from him, and went back and stood by the bank of the Jordan. Then he took the mantle of Elijah that had fallen from him, and struck the water, and said, 'Where is the LORD God of Elijah?' And when he also had struck the water, it was divided this way and that; and Elisha crossed over."

Upon seeing Elijah lifted up towards the heavens Elisha breaks forth with a mighty praise report for he sees his father taken up into Heaven. No, Elijah was not his natural father. However, he was his spiritual father and that meant something to Elijah that his father was being taken from him. The comment "the chariot of Israel and its horsemen" refers to angelic activity being dispatched from God and being sent to gather Elijah.

Finally, brothers and sisters, let me share the proof that if a mentor/protégé relationship abides in the knowledge that if the mentor would do it so should the protégé. Notice when Elisha does his first miracle. Before he does anything physically he does something spiritually. He reaches out to God. He says, "Where is the LORD God of Elijah?" We know that Elijah's God was Elisha's God and it was proven by the miracle. Notice, he does exactly what Elijah did. He rolled up the mantle, just like his mentor, and he smote the water, just like his mentor.

The failed priests who refused to travel with them across the Jordan knew that God's authority abided with Elisha. " Now when the sons of the prophets who were from Jericho saw him, they said, 'The spirit of Elijah rests on Elisha.' And they came to meet him, and bowed to the ground before him."

The Spirit of God rested on Elisha because Elisha was willing to pay the price that others were not. I think back to the times when I was a young minister just starting out in ministry and I would always wonder how I would stack up against the other preachers. During the years, I have kept up with some of them, and I find it sad to say that many men who were truly gifted in God turned their backs on Him because they were not willing to pay the price for true ministry.

Over the years, I have sat under several mighty men of God. I have served in Baptist churches, Full Gospel Baptist churches, C.O.G.I.C. churches, as well as non-denominational churches, and I must say that all of them have rubbed off on me in various ways. I believe of all the churches that I have served under, the spirit of two of my mentors rests on me. It cannot be truly defined, but I know that when I operate as they did it empowers me to preach stronger, to preach with more clarity, and to preach with conviction.

If you are in a mentor/protégé relationship, continue until God separates you. Even though I am now a pastor, I am also a mentor, and I still talk regularly with my former pastors and mentors. When God calls them home to glory it will be a sad day, but I know God has a purpose for us all.

It is with that same knowledge that I try to train and inspire as many sons and daughters in the ministry that I can. Some I will simply guide. Others I will train. However, for the few, the one or maybe two gifted ministers who travel with me, it is my prayer that one day they will be able to catch the mantle of leadership and guide the church into the next level of God.

Study Guide

Chapter 6: Passing the Mantle of Leadership

1. We all suffer droughts, famines, and pestilences in our ministry. What helps you survive these areas? What are some of the things God has taught you to sustain yourself in these seasons?

2. Have you ever been truly fearful in ministry? Have you heard Jezebel's voice and decided that ministry is too taxing for you? Have you ever declared your own benediction and end of your ministry? How do you think God saw you in the moment you tried to give up?

3. Have you ever had an experience like Elijah in the cave? What did God say to you in your cave that convinced you to keep trying? What was the central fact that caused you to give ministry another chance?

4. As a young Elisha, are you mature enough to follow your leader through the rigors of ministry and still be able to praise God when he receives his reward? Are you strong enough to serve him and see him in his strong times as well as in his weak times and still support him with your best service?

5. What mantle of God are you currently walking in? Look over your time serving your Elijah. Do you see yourself worthy to carry their mantle? Why or why not?

CONCLUSION

Thank you for taking this journey with me.

What you have read in the preceding pages is what God gave to me in my personal life.

They are steps that I had to take to learn the "why" of my life and the reasons the Lord chose such a worthless case to use in sharing His name.

As I am still a work on His wheel, in the most humble spirit, I thank Him for all of His blessings, and I thank Him for every day of my life.

Child of God, God's will is perfect. You may have gone through some very rough times in your life, but God brought you through. Now, He wants to use your life for His purpose.

I pray that you will let Him in.

Father, I ask right now, that You touch my friend reading this book, that You will show them that everything that has happened in their lives has been inside Your will. I know they might be hurt and damaged, but I ask You to give them the strength to climb on Your wheel and be re-created in Your likeness. I pray that You will bless them, sanctify them for Your purpose, and use them to be a light in this world. I thank You for each and every one who will call on Your name, and I pray that You will lead and guide them into a better revelation of whom and what You are to them. In Jesus' name, Amen.

DECISION FOR CHRIST

For the Unsaved:

The decision to accept Jesus Christ as your Lord and Savior is the most important decision you will ever make. You'll experience purpose, peace, joy, and a secured eternity in Heaven through your relationship with Christ. Pray this prayer and accept Christ as your Lord and Savior.

"Heavenly Father, Your Word says that 'if I believe in my heart and confess with my mouth that Jesus Christ is the son of God I will be saved.' Father, I am a sinner. But I believe in Jesus Christ as my Savior. I believe that Jesus died to pay for my sins and then rose from the grave for me. I accept You into my life. I turn from doing things my way. I give You total control of my life as I submit my will to Yours. Thank You for saving me and giving me new life. Amen."

If you would like to contact us please write to us at:

Dr. Rayford E. Malone Ministries

Cell: 214-676-0050

Or email us at: Ray.Malone.Books@gmail.com